PRAISE FOR RE]

RED SKY gives us a textured glimpse into t
world of Manila in the immediate aften.__
experienced by an intrepid young American mariner who liked to
live perilously close to the sharp edge. Phil Mehan's exploits and
misadventures, portrayed by two bestselling authors who know the
Philippines well, make for fascinating reading—while affording us a
seldom-seen perspective of what was really happening in this farthest
corner of the American Empire once the guns of war fell silent.

—Hampton Sides, author of *Ghost Soldiers*

By the middle of page one I knew I was reading something well-
researched, well-crafted – comparable to "Shogun," "The Bridge
Over the River Kwai," or "The Bourne Identity." Set in post-WW2
Manila when anti-communist paranoia was exploited by power-crazed
espionage agents, this action thriller is the true story of Phil Mehan,
a suave merchant marine officer in his early twenties. Staying in war-
torn Manila as a civilian shipping agent, Mehan was strangely arrested,
jailed in infamous Bilibad Prison, then incredibly escaped to discover
that he'd been framed as a spy and gun-runner for communist forces
in the Philippines. As Mehan evades the man-hunt for him, he knows
he ought to flee home to the USA. But he still thinks he can "Beat
the Devil at his own game," and make a fortune in the Philippines.
Unaware that his every move is being monitored by murderous
intelligence agents of the American "G2" counter-intelligence corps,
his very life is in grave danger. This incredible but true story is one
you won't be able to put down.

--Dan Traub, Dreamkeeper Films, Hollywood

Phil's imprisonment at Bilibad prison and his escape is miraculous. I
recommend this book for all history buffs and entrepreneurs.

--Everett D. Reamer, Bataan vet and torture survivor

RED SKY
in the morning

The secret history of two men who got away

-- and one who didn't.

A Bowstring Book

A Bowstring Book <www.bowstring.net>
Booksurge Publishing
Copyright © 2008 Sterling & Peggy Seagrave
Cover design by Ultrafina.com

British Library Cataloguing in Publication Data
A catalogue record for this book is available from the British Library

Library of Congress Cataloguing in Publication Data
A catalogue record for this book is available from the Library of Congress

ISBN: 1-4392-4047-7
ISBN-13: 9781439240472

Visit www.booksurge.com to order additional copies

Dedicated to
Iris and Philip Mehan,
who gave us access to letters,
diaries, memories, family archives,
and previously secret G-2 documents
to solve a mystery that had baffled them for a lifetime

—

Readers who would like to examine more of the
G-2 Surveillance Documents may find them at
<phil-iris.com>

A Bowstring Book <www.bowstring.net>

Booksurge Publishing

Other books by
Sterling & Peggy Seagrave

———————

GOLD WARRIORS

THE YAMATO DYNASTY

LORDS OF THE RIM

DRAGON LADY

THE MARCOS DYNASTY

THE SOONG DYNASTY

BUSH PILOTS

SOLDIERS OF FORTUNE

YELLOW RAIN

RED SKY
in the morning

. . .

Mariner's Saying:

Red Sky at night, sailors' delight.

Red Sky in the morning, sailors' warning.

TABLE OF CONTENTS

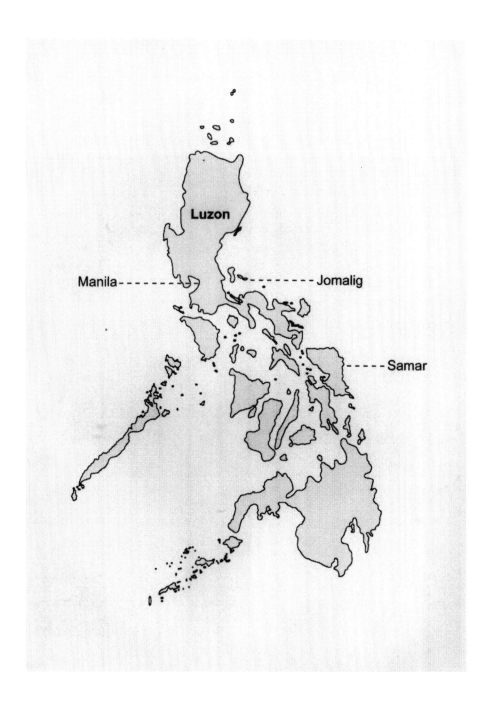

THE PHILIPPINES

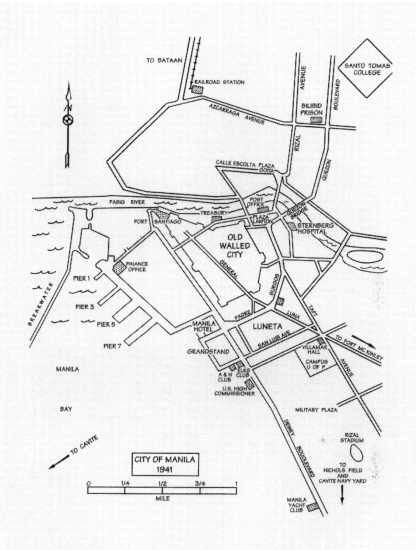

TO BATAAN

RAILROAD STATION

AZCARRAGA AVENUE

AVENUE

SANTO TOMAS
COLLEGE

BILIBID
PRISON

RIZAL

QUEZON

BOULEVARD

CALLE ESCOLTA PLAZA
GOITA

N

PASIG RIVER

TREASURY

POST
OFFICE

QUEZON
BRIDGE

PLAZA
LAWTON

STERNBERG
HOSPITAL

FORT SANTIAGO

OLD
WALLED
CITY

FINANCE
OFFICE

PIER 1

GENERAL

BURGOS

PIER 3

PIER 5

LUNA

TAFT

PADRE

MANILA
HOTEL

LUNETA

TO FORT MC KINLEY

PIER 7

GRANDSTAND

SAN LUIS AVE

VILLAMAR
HALL

AVENUE

BREAKWATER

MANILA

A & N
CLUB

ELKS
CLUB

CAMPUS
U OF P

U.S. HIGH
COMMISSIONER

BAY

MILITARY PLAZA

DEWEY

RIZAL
STADIUM

TO CAVITE

BOULEVARD

TO
NICHOLS FIELD
AND
CAVITE NAVY YARD

CITY OF MANILA
1941

0   1/4   1/2   3/4   1

MILE

MANILA
YACHT
CLUB

CENTRAL MANILA

Authors' Note

Magellan's Folly

The great Portuguese explorer Ferdinand Magellan is famous for two things: Setting out on what became the first voyage around the world – and for getting himself killed under ridiculous circumstances before the voyage was over. After reaching what we now call The Philippines, Magellan was given a warm welcome by villagers, but could not resist boasting about the power of his ship's cannons, and the military might of his conquistadores. His host said, "In that case, please show us your might by putting down the evil warlord called Lapu-Lapu who has been attacking us with his private army." Thinking it would be easy, Magellan vowed to do so. His plan was to bring his fighting ships close enough to bombard Lapu-Lapu's stronghold on the nearby island called Mactan. Before dawn on April 27, 1521, as he brought his ships silently up to the curved bay of Mactan Island, Magellan realized with dread that he had committed an act of colossal folly. Rocks prevented his warships from entering the small bay close enough to bombard the town. Forfeiting the advantage of his ships' cannons, he should have abandoned his plan and simply sailed off into the red sunrise, to everlasting glory. Instead, rashly hoping to catch Lapu-Lapu off guard, Magellan and 49 men waded barelegged hundreds of yards to the beach, where they were charged by some 1,500 native warriors armed with spears and clubs. *"Our men fled, while only six or eight of us remained with our captain. The warriors threw spears at our bare legs. We were helpless to defend ourselves. As a good captain and a knight, Magellan stood fast. A native stabbed him in the face with a lance. Trying to reach his own sword, the captain could only draw it half way. Seeing this, all the warriors threw themselves upon him, piercing his leg with a lance, whereby he fell face down. They all rushed upon him with lances of iron and bamboo, so that they slew our mirror, our comfort, and our true guide."*

- **Antonio Pigafeta, Magellan's Venetian chronicler, writing to the king of Spain.**

1

Prologue :

GOOD MORNING, MAGELLAN !

At first light on September 29, 1945, the U.S. Army transport EVANGELINE entered Manila Bay with Corregidor Island to port, and the dense rainforest of Bataan Peninsula beyond. Leaning on the taffrail, 21-year-old Phil Mehan drank in the beauty and fragrance of Paradise. Like Magellan, who had discovered The Philippines for Spain four centuries earlier, Phil saw himself as a born navigator; a natural. Both survived typhoons, shifting sandbars, and zero visibility in the Pacific Ocean and the China Sea. Both learned the hard way that navigating on land among devious predatory humans is far more deadly in The Philippines, which looks like Paradise but often functions like Purgatory. Magellan was given a friendly welcome to these lush islands, only to be stabbed and beaten to death by the warriors of Dato Lapu-Lapu (Lord Grouper, after the big fish). Phil and one of his two friends and business partners escaped a similar death only by sheer luck and quick wits, as the evil spirit of Lapu-Lapu struck again. How he escaped from Manila police detectives, prison guards, underworld thugs, Filipino secret police, agents of U.S. Army Counter-Intelligence, and U.S. Military Police, both in The Philippines and in China, not to mention a few angry young women, would have amused Houdini and Don Juan. What happened to the third partner, a charming but vulnerable White Russian emigre they called Cheez, was not funny. He was one of the first victims of the Cold War and its anti-communist death squads, and did not get away.

Being only a kid, and a hard-headed one at that, Phil would spend two years in The Philippines before realizing there was a pattern to the bad things happening, and that he was marked for death. Like Magellan he should have fled immediately but, again like Magellan, he thought he could beat the devil. The trick lay in knowing who the devil was.

At first, Phil thought his problems were the result of a bad business deal made by a company that hired him and his friends to prepare five U.S. Army surplus freighters for delivery from Manila to Shanghai. The purchase of the freighters was foolishly done, enabling the U.S. Army to choose its worst ships, and to drag its feet in making them seaworthy.

Phil also thought he was being victimized by gangsters in the Filipino Seamen's Union whose captains and crews played tricks and made endless trouble. Meantime, Phil also managed to enrage the manager of the elegant Manila Hotel, who was a member of the ruling Filipino elite and personal friend of General Douglas MacArthur. To be sure, Phil did provoke many problems simply by acting like Zorro. After all, he was only 21. What he never guessed was that he and his friends were also under scrutiny by the U.S. Army Counter-Intelligence Corps (G-2), which reported to General MacArthur, and the Pentagon, generating a two-foot-tall collection of Top Secret surveillance documents called the Project Manila File. Half a century passed, then two-thirds of the file was laundered for reasons of 'national security' and the remaining 300 pages were declassified and sent to the U.S. National Archives where they were discovered by a researcher.

The moving force behind Project Manila was a man who later became one of the CIA's top-guns – General Edward Lansdale, whose career as a Cold Warrior began in Manila, before moving on to assassination plots and death squads in Saigon, Tokyo, Guatemala, Havana, and Dallas. Lansdale was only getting warmed up in Manila, a former ad-agency copy writer learning how to provoke the dogs of war. In the story that follows, it is Lansdale who takes on the role of Lapu-Lapu, the Big Fish. The Project Manila File compiled by his deputies puts an entirely different spin on the innocent folly of Phil and his friends. In astonishing detail, it documents every move they made in those two years, every letter, telegram, radiogram, phone call, coming and going, to whom they spoke in a hotel lobby, how much they spent on a bar tab, whom they met in nightclubs, and what their role was as "a top-secret Soviet spy ring" that Lansdale insisted was financing terror and revolution in The Philippines. All this was triggered when Phil was joined in Manila by the young White Russian Vadim Chirskoff -- 'Cheez' -- who would become the main target of Lansdale's messianic crusade.

So this story has two narrative threads: The folly of Phil and his pals as they blundered into traps placed in their path, and the spiderwork of central government power misused by Lansdale in pursuit of personal wealth and a global career. What begins as a picaresque misadventure becomes a bitter cautionary tale, on how political agendas turn innocence into tragedy.

Phil was no more naive than other young Americans who enlisted toward the end of the war, like the baby turtles that hatch at night on Pacific beaches, and try to scramble into the water before they are snapped up by whirling seabirds. But he was born defiant. Others would play billiards carefully, but Phil would smash the cue-ball as hard as he could, expecting to sink two or three balls by sheer audacity. His Christian upbringing in California had been strict, though he quickly learned to bend rules without breaking them. Like many Americans, his first life-lessons came from comic books. "I believed I could do anything, like Superman. I could be an instant hero." Trim and fit from training as an amateur boxer, 5-feet 11-inches, weighing 170 pounds, with dark brown hair, he bore a resemblance to the wolfish young Errol Flynn, drawing attention from young women. Phil was still a virgin, did not smoke or swear, and drank only soda pop. But he wanted everyone to think he played with fire. When he was first drafted at age 18, in March 1943, "I frankly hadn't given much thought to the war." But it was great to be free from parental restrictions. His first letter home from Army boot-camp announced that he had learned to make a bed.

Most of his comrades also were experiencing freedom for the first time. They now had no one to smell their breath or check their wallets for condoms. Curfews set by a foul-mouthed Army sergeant were easier to evade than those of loving parents.

For all his foxiness, Phil was offended by basic training at Fort Knox, Kentucky, where recruits were greeted by Army skinheads with bullying and blasphemy, delivered with spittle: "Maybe your heart belongs to Jesus, but, by God, your ass belongs to me!"

Phil saw that discipline was being used to degrade farm boys, grocery clerks, college students, and day-dreamers, to turn them into robots, so they could be turned into soldiers. He had been raised on American ideals of individuality and personal rights, so he decided to fight back. Refusing to conform, he made himself a target of his platoon sergeant, who decided Phil was too handsome, too cocky, and too smart-assed. Phil rose to the challenge by trying harder and doing better, infuriating the sergeant who rightly saw this precision as a calculated affront. After a month of basic training, the recruits were bussed to Louisville for a dance with local girls set up by the United Service Organization. Phil and a buddy were invited instead to a going-away party for a Colonel

Thompson, at the Thompson family home in Mockingbird Valley. The colonel himself drove them back to Louisville, arriving too late to catch the Army busses back to base. Stranded, they spent the night sleeping on tables in a pool hall. When they got back to base next day, Phil's explanation was rejected by his sergeant, and he was given a work detail at the base laundry, and the base kitchen, the same weekend.

"I couldn't be two places at once, so I reported to the laundry." His platoon sergeant had enough. He transferred Phil to a unit about to be sent overseas. Waiting for their orders to come through, the unit was kept busy loading railway freight cars with ammunition. To avoid such tedium, Phil hid under his bunk, and decided it was time to use his flat feet to talk his way into 'Limited Service' inside the U.S. Nobody in the Army was fooled by the flat-foot excuse -- it merely served to identify enlistees who would use any means to avoid obeying orders. The decision on these claims rested with a review panel headed by a colonel, who noted that Phil had gone through basic training with no complaints.

"So how is it that, faced with going overseas, your feet start bothering you?"

Phil replied: "Sir, I was determined to serve my country overseas so I didn't complain during basic. Now it appears I'll be put in Limited Service, unable to serve overseas. I'd prefer to leave the Army completely so I can join the Merchant Marine, where flat-feet won't keep me from overseas duty."

Concluding that Phil was a hard case, the colonel said with heavy irony, "I wish there were more men like you." In August 1943, five months after being drafted, Phil received an honorable discharge, and went home to California.

He was vaguely serious about joining the merchant marine's Army Transport Corps -- not to avoid overseas duty but to avoid platoon sergeants.

There was no hurry, so he spent the next four months working night-shift at a shipyard in San Pedro, alongside his father, building Liberty ships and Victory ships. The assembly line was vast. Giant components were fabricated in shops around the harbor, then brought to dry-docks, where men welded their plates together. But it was boring, so he kept his promise to join the Merchant Marine.

Compared to Army boot camp, Merchant Marine training in Catalina Island, St. Petersburg and New Orleans was a cakewalk. Phil graduated as a Lieutenant Junior Grade, and was assigned to LITTLE EVA for his first journey outside the United States. He started as a Junior Third Mate in the Army Transport Corps or ATC, which hauled soldiers and equipment back and forth. As one of America's 'ninety-day-wonders' trained in haste, he missed combat by only six-weeks, and was now part of easygoing Operation Magic Carpet. On outbound trips, Magic Carpet took fresh personnel and supplies to Asia to help in reconstruction. On homeward voyages, the same ships carried home battle-weary GI's and American civilians liberated from four years of Japanese occupation.

LITTLE EVA, as the crew called her, was a 5,000-ton cruise ship built in 1927 for the Eastern Steamship Lines of Boston, to serve as a Honeymoon Special carrying love-smitten passengers on one-night coastal cruises. With the outbreak of war in 1941, she had been hastily refitted as a troop transport on the Atlantic run, carrying more than a thousand soldiers packed like anchovies. Now she was on the Manila run.

Phil's first sight of Manila was a shock. LITTLE EVA dropped anchor in front of a seawall lined with bomb-splintered palms. The city, once beautiful, was a scene of near total destruction. Most buildings had been flattened, or stood like broken molars.

The exception was the undamaged Manila Hotel in what once had been a verdant park near the waterfront.

"Manila Harbor is a mess," he wrote home, "littered with masts and smokestacks of sunken ships."

The rubble teemed with humanity, as survivors scavenged to keep flesh on their protruding bones.

"These people are very much in need of food," Phil wrote. "Every day we put the garbage out on the dock, and gangs of Filipinos ransack it, salvaging everything imaginable." When he got shore leave to explore the devastated city, he found that luxuries such as a shoe-shine, or malted milk, which cost five or ten cents in California, were ten times that price.

Back on board his ship, he watched GIs and WACs laughing as they crowded onto LITTLE EVA. "Our combat troops are just crying to get home. We are taking aboard some 400 WACs, about 600 GIs and a considerable number of officers. You should see the expressions on their faces as they come up the gangplank, a happier bunch you never could see."

After sailing back to San Francisco on LITTLE EVA with her cargo of exhausted soldiers and weary WACs, Phil was sent to Fort Mason in San Francisco for reassignment. His new ship was the transport USS ADMIRAL HUGHES, returning to Manila, where the great misadventure of his life would begin.

Chapter 1 :

RUNNING THE CONVENT

Filipinos joke that after Magellan they spent 400 years locked up in a Spanish convent, followed by 50 years in an American brothel. For them the Japanese occupation was only the latest in a series of misfortunes.

Like other Spanish colonies, The Philippines had been a Catholic theocracy, but behind the prayers and incense its rulers were interested less in heavenly estate than real estate. Like the friars who came with them, they arrived without women and made temporary arrangements with local girls who produced prodigious numbers of mestizo babies. Raised as good Catholics, they could own land and engage in business, but were snubbed for 'impurities of blood'. Yet as more land came under mestizo ownership, they turned against their pure-bred masters in 1869 and plotted revolution. Spain replied by executing the wrong man -- the poet Jose Rizal -- who was not involved. His execution drove the whole country into rebellion. Just as Filipinos gained the upper hand, America butted in. The U.S. was in a deep depression, its politicians looking for a way to distract their angry citizens. War with a weak Spain was the quick fix, provoked by sinking the battleship USS MAINE in Havana harbor, which galvanized Americans against Madrid. As the Spanish Philippines were poorly defended, President McKinley sent Admiral George Dewey's Pacific Fleet with ten thousand Yankee troops experienced in massacring red indians. On May 1, 1898, Dewey defeated the Spanish fleet in Manila Bay without losing a single man. Filipinos vainly hoped that America would support them in throwing off colonial rule. Instead, President McKinley paid Spain $21-million to acquire the islands for America, and Yankee troops began exterminating Filipinos they referred to contemptuously as 'goo-goos' while turning the islands into a 'howling wilderness'. By 1900, two-thirds of the U.S. Army were fighting in The Philippines. More than a million Filipinos died. By comparison, during the Japanese occupation of The Philippines in World War II, only 147,000 soldiers and civilians died.

Confronted by this new tyranny, Filipino landowners -- mestizo, Iberian, or Chinese -- decided wealth was more important than freedom, so they got in bed with the Yankees, and rose quickly to political power.

Among them were the Quezons, Quirinos, Laurels, and Aquinos. Fighting ceased, and The Philippines became an American plaything. The first colonial governor was 300-pound William Howard Taft.

Taft assembled a genial collaboration between rich men on both sides, who together controlled 90 percent of the islands' wealth, profiting hugely from exports of tobacco, sugar, and tropical fruit. In return, the Filipino elite guaranteed their support of American policy. Democratic rule became a well-oiled pretense.

In the countryside, where great estates had been established by Catholic priests, rich Overseas Chinese families took over, thinly disguised by Filipinized names, like the Cojuangcos. They owned most of the arable land around Manila, which they ruled with private armies. Outer islands including Mindanao became the domains of giant U.S. corporations like Dole. On the eve of World War II, all Filipinos were promised independence. But they would have to endure four years of Japanese brutality before that day would come.

The two most powerful faction leaders on the main island of Luzon were Manuel Quezon who headed the puppet colonial government, and Elpidio Quirino, who headed an underworld machine that did his and Quezon's dirty work, and controlled every commodity including tobacco, sugar, and human flesh. Quirino's Ilocano mafia took its name from the northwest coastal regions called Ilocos Norte and Ilocos Sur. As the only part of The Philippines that was hardscrabble brown, rather than verdant green, the two Ilocano provinces spawned men as merciless as the mafiosi of Sicily or Corsica.

Together, Quezon and Quirino dominated the puppet regime that rose to power following the American takeover. When General Arthur MacArthur became their governor-general, his son Douglas was assigned to his father's command on graduation from West Point. Over four tours of duty in Manila, young Douglas MacArthur became 'brothers' with President Quezon, and set the love-hate pattern for all the elite to follow. It is hardly surprising then, that Filipinos from top to bottom had mixed feelings about their American masters. Servitude is a tough habit to shake.

Among themselves, Filipino oligarchs assured each other that this subservience was only a pretense, until the country was free and could get off its back and on its feet.

Briefly in 1945, Americans were welcomed back to Manila as liberators, rather than colonial oppressors. In only a few months, however, as soldiers were once again displaced by a new wave of Yankee carpet-baggers, sentiment again turned against the masters.

As independence approached in 1946, everyone was on the make: masters, middlemen, and serfs. The U.S. War Damage Commission in Manila, set up to dispose of surplus U.S. military equipment in Operation Roll-Up, became a notorious conduit for scams, bribery, and kickbacks. Millions of dollars in new consumer goods arrived in the Philippines for the maintenance of the occupying U.S. Army and Navy. Practically overnight, one quarter of these goods ended up on the black market. Temptations were too great to do otherwise. U.S. officials, Filipino politicians, bureaucrats, lawyers and police, worked with GIs to hijack Jeeps, trucks, powdered milk, pistols, clothing, typewriters, cigarettes, booze, medicines, PT-boats. Senior military officers allied themselves with the Quirino Machine or rival gangs in selling surplus Liberty ships, Victory ships, and smaller coastal freighters called F-boats. As these ships went through the process of being decommissioned by the military, they were stripped of nearly everything, and the bare hulls sold on to unsuspecting buyers. If you drove a hard bargain, the Army would re-equip the vessel and make it seaworthy, but the Army officers involved were not saints. Fortunes were made overnight by men who had once been part of famous combat units like the Flying Tigers, Merrill's Marauders, OSS 101, or the Office of Naval Intelligence.

Being little more than a kid, Phil knew nothing of this cosy club of high-rollers, Filipino and American, or he might have thought twice about seeking his fortune here. He had yet to meet certain people who would bring him into direct contact with the overlords. These would include romancing Nena Nieto, the beautiful daughter of tobacco millionaire Colonel Manuel Nieto, personal aide to the late President Quezon, personal friend of General MacArthur, and personal ally of godfather Quirino. When Phil met Nena Nieto at the swimming pool of the Manila Hotel, his problems would multiply. Getting into Paradise was easy. But getting out alive was another matter.

Chapter 2 :

AN IMPERFECT STORM

On his return to Manila aboard the ADMIRAL HUGHES, Phil's lazy life on the Magic Carpet Run came to an abrupt end when he was transferred to be first mate on one of the surplus freighters being refitted in the U.S. Army shipyard at Cavite, on the bay just south of Manila. The FS-261 was one of many ships sold recently to the Nationalist Chinese government, to haul guns and men up the Yangtze for the climax of the civil war between Generalissimo Chiang and Chairman Mao.

Her new owners re-named the ship the PEONY which, along with plum-blossoms, are China's national flowers. Compared to most surplus freighters being sold cheap to Asian allies, PEONY was in excellent shape; she had been in service less than a year. One of 318 coastal freighters built for the U.S. Army during World War II, 180 feet over all, displacing 560 tons, she had been commissioned late in the war at the Wheeler yard in New York. Her famous sister was the USS PUEBLO, a CIA electronic spy ship that would be captured by North Korea in 1968 -- still on display today in Pyongyang -- the first U.S. Navy ship to be hijacked on the high seas by a foreign military force.

Phil was responsible for making PEONY look good before delivering her to the Chinese government in Shanghai. He and a chief engineer were to supervise her refitting without anyone looking over their shoulders. He could not complain. With the war over, many men were resigning from the Army Transport Corps and going home, creating opportunities for ambitious youngsters. Overnight, he jumped in rank from Third Mate to First Mate. Although peace had ended some war-risk bonuses, and other perks, a First Mate earned much more than a Third.

Enjoying life, salting money away, were the only things on his mind:

"In the Pacific I could build a hefty nest-egg. My officer's pay was now $3,102.00 a year, plus a month's pay for annual leave and expenses, and another $2 per day for war zone pay. All tax-free." (In 1946, $1 was equivalent to $13 today.)

Every sailor since Jonah knew Sod's Law: "If it can go wrong, it will go wrong." So, having a gifted engineer aboard ship was crucial. Phil got off on the wrong foot with PEONY's engineer, Robert Peterson.

"The first day I reported aboard PEONY there was no one on deck. Deciding to take charge, I went to the wheelhouse and started fiddling with the engine room telegraph, clanking it forward and backward, sending noisy signals down to the engine-room. Next thing I knew, a man armed with two .45 automatics stormed into the wheelhouse looking for the 'GD, SOB, MFing idiot' who had disturbed his nap. As I later learned, Peterson was gun-happy, and I was lucky that he didn't shoot the 'idiot' right then and there." Instead, the two became fast friends.

Peterson was handsome in a way rarely seen off fashion catwalks. His face was square-jawed and rugged, his dark hair neatly combed back from an intelligent brow, and his brown eyes had that kind of direct gaze magazine photographers seek. Solidly built at five foot ten, he had a natural grace and a negligent swagger. In one photo, dressed in camel-hair coat and jodhpurs with aviator's boots, a pretty girl on each arm, he has the air of a World War I flying ace, just back in his Sopwith Camel from a joust with the Red Baron. None of this gave a hint of Pete's poverty stricken childhood during the Great Depression in a Pennsylvania farming town in the coal belt, where he and ten siblings judged the size of a meal by counting the beans on their plates. This hard edge stayed with him, making him wildly unpredictable, a bit brutal. His obsession with guns and engines suited him well when he escaped the backwoods by joining the Merchant Marine, assigned to ATC freighters in the Pacific.

The war was his ticket out of poverty, but one of his ships was attacked, exploded and sank with most of his comrades; Pete survived the sinking and afterward was constantly wary. At the end of the war he decided to stay in the Pacific, continuing with the ATC as an engineer at Cavite working on the PEONY's engine. He could not have been less like Phil, but they formed a durable bond that passed for solid friendship. They were the same age but, like a slightly older brother, Pete would come to Phil's rescue more than once.

Guns and temper aside, Pete's common sense and his credentials as an engineering wizard guaranteed jobs wherever he went. He now ranked as a chief engineer and appreciated the wages and security. He had now been with the ATC long enough so he could quit any time he wished. With only the two of them aboard around the clock, Pete quickly adjusted to Phil's endless pranks and eccentricities.

When ships were refurbished at Cavite, they were normally given a quick coat of battleship grey, top to bottom. Phil decided to give PEONY a real facelift to suit her new name. He thought it would impress his superiors and lead to bigger and better things.

"We could use any color of paint we wanted," he said, "as long it was grey." But grey comes in many shades and tints. On his watch, PEONY would become the prettiest girl at the prom.

He had bargaining chips. Each month, the ATC provided two cases of beer plus cartons of cigarettes to each man. As a non-drinker and non-smoker, Phil used his beer and butts for barter. When he heard that bright blue-grey paint was available for the right price, he traded his rations to the owner of the paint and put his crew of Filipinos to work brush PEONY's hull.

"I painted the hull blue-grey. It will look even better after I get the super-structure painted light grey."

When PEONY was nearly ready for sea, she was put under the command of Captain Eriksen, an American of Scandinavian origin who completed their triangle of camaraderie.

Phil, the teetotaler, decided Eriksen was "a swell fellow at sea, but he drank a lot when in port". Eriksen was a giant of a man with unruly blond hair and ice-blue eyes, over six feet tall and 210 pounds, work-calloused hands, fingers stained yellow by his chain smoking. At age 40 he seemed old to Phil, but he had the physique, mind-set, and appetites of a Viking accustomed to drinking his way through interminable Nordic nights. And he did not like drinking alone. Phil solved the problem by downing a tomato juice for every whisky the skipper knocked back. Eriksen always ended up under the table. Fortunately PEONY's tables were bolted down.

Pete was not always around when help was needed, as when Phil borrowed PEONY's motor launch to go ship-hopping for goodies.

"I jumped into the launch and cast-off without starting the motor. The engine then refused to start. With a dead-engine, I couldn't control the launch, and the outgoing tide carried me toward the harbor mouth at terrific speed. With hundreds of ships anchored in Cavite harbor, the only thing in real danger was my dignity. I gestured frantically to Captain Eriksen, who simply laughed and waved goodbye."

These were still golden days for Americans in Manila. What could not be bought was available by barter. A hustler could make a fortune on the black market. Captain Eriksen had a real knack for hustling captains of cargo ships arriving heavy-laden from the U.S. He invited them to cocktails aboard PEONY, climaxing with a drinking contest and a game of dice.

Visiting captains wagered part of their cargoes of fresh meat, milk and other luxuries. No one was counting. Eriksen never let on that he used loaded dice.

"Inevitably, Eriksen won and we all enjoyed the spoils at dinner." These were bacchanals of fresh beef, lumpy mashed potatoes, greasy gravy and sliced white bread – the only thing missing was a wench to pour the ale.

Before PEONY could leave for Shanghai, Peterson had to get both its diesels running smoothly. One was fine, but the other had problems. An Australian chief engineer on a neighboring ship offered to help. The Ozzie thought he knew more about diesels than Doctor Diesel himself, and wasn't shy about it. After a brief discussion on deck, Pete, two crewmen, and the Ozzie went below to the engine room. Phil was on a nearby wharf, tying up a dingy, when he heard muffled explosions. Looking out at PEONY, he saw smoke billowing from her spit-shined portholes.

Rowing back as fast as he could, Phil was met by black smoke and blue curses. The soot-smeared Ozzie was scrambling frantically down a rope-work Jacob's ladder, jumped into his own dingy and put as much distance between himself and PEONY as possible. Her engine had gone berserk. A runaway engine can quickly turn into a bomb, threatening not only to sink the ship but kill the crew.

Like many ships laid-up for months, or in mothballs, PEONY's fuel-lines had been shut down. But a mothballed engine can start running just on oil sucked out of its crankcase, or vapors from anti-rust treatments. Some of PEONY's fuel injectors leaked diesel into the cylinders, and the extra fuel had ignited suddenly when the Ozzie and Pete got the motor started. The engine was now racing into the red-line, ready to throw its rods and explode.

As the Ozzie fled, Peterson raced to the storeroom, donned a gas mask, and grabbed blankets and a fire extinguisher. Dashing back down the slippery steel ladders, he hosed down the engine with fire-extinguisher, then threw the blankets over it to starve the motor of air. Pete had put his life on the line. Asked why the Ozzie had left in such a hurry, Pete shrugged: "He didn't say, but I guess it scared hell out of him."

That problem solved, PEONY was soon ready to hoist anchor. She would join a convoy of five similar surplus ships, plus several PT-boats also being handed over to the Nationalist Chinese. In charge of the entire convoy aboard its lead ship was a Captain Martin, who loved women the way Eriksen loved whisky.

Normally, the convoy would make the trip from Manila to Shanghai in six or seven days. But with Sod's Law and Captain Martin calling the shots, the voyage turned into a sexual odyssey lasting three weeks.

Once out of Manila Bay, heading north along the west coast of Luzon, the first sign all was not going according to plan came when Captain Martin took the convoy into Gaang Bay's idyllic harbor and anchored off the picturesque town of Currimao. The town got its name in Spanish days when Moslem pirates were an ever-present danger. Juan de Salcedo, a conquistador who found the harbor in 1572 and claimed it for the king of Spain, christened his small fort Currimao by combining "run" (curri) from the "moors" (mao).

There Captain Martin's convoy remained anchored four days, while their crews exchanged food, cigarettes and other small luxuries for the favors of local women and girls, or simply to have their clothes washed and mended. While wives and daughters were aboard slaking the crews' lust, the local men kept busy scrubbing decks, chipping and painting. To counter questions from headquarters about deviating from their assigned course, Captain Martin sent wires saying bad weather had forced them to seek refuge. This seemed to provoke the weather gods.

From Gaang Bay, the physically spent crews moved their ships north toward Taiwan, whereupon one of PEONY's engines started misfiring from a defective fuel filter. Refuge was found this time at Kaohsiung on the southwestern tip of Formosa. This was lucky as most of the crew was in need of medical attention, thanks to the girls.

At least they were now technically in China. A Japanese colony for 50 years from 1895-1945, Formosa had been returned to Chinese rule, the name Taiwan restored, as part of the terms of Japan's surrender. Here was a beautiful big island with a towering mountain range and a colorful history of pirates and rebels. Most famous of all was a half-Chinese, half-Japanese giant called Coxinga, who had many things in common with Alexander the Great. Back in the 17th century, Coxinga had tried to seize mainland China from its Manchu usurpers, to re-establish the previous Ming dynasty. After many victories, his ambitions were ended prematurely when he was bitten by one of Taiwan's mosquitos and died in agony of cerebral malaria.

In all, the convoy was at Kaohsiung for a week. The crews occupied themselves with trading, sightseeing and whoring. Phil, taken 'sightseeing' by Captain Martin, ended up with four other men at a luxurious brothel where they were fed, bathed and over-nighted. Girls included, even if you abstained, the total bill for five came only to 7-cents U.S.

The waterfront turned into a bazaar as locals came to trade with the crews. Everything from silks to abandoned Samurai swords were exchanged for cigarettes and chewing gum.

While in Kaohsiung, the convoy acquired a passenger, a Spanish priest who had been stranded in Taiwan during World War II. Because of his faltering English it was difficult to understand all his adventures, but it was clear he saw his missionary work as a failure. It was agreed to give the disillusioned priest passage to Shanghai, on his way back to Spain.

With PEONY's fuel system repaired, sexually-transmitted diseases dealt with, and rough weather clearing up, the convoy again headed out for Shanghai. But, once again, they did not get far:

"That evening we encountered another severe storm and the convoy returned to Kaohsiung. We did not know it at the time, but Typhoon Barbara was coming, while we spent three more days in harbor." This delay nearly cost the convoy ships and men. Captain Martin, under mounting pressure to get the convoy to Shanghai, would now take risks to compensate for time squandered in the brothels of Currimao and Kaohsiung.

Two days after leaving Kaohsiung the second time, tropical storm warnings were again received. Martin decided the weather would hold until the convoy was beyond the storm's predicted path. Wrong once again. By late afternoon the barometer was falling, while wind and sea were rising.

"By nightfall," Phil recalls, "we were in hell." Typhoon Barbara had struck.

It was early in the year for a typhoon. Typhoon Barbara -- the first of 1946 -- arrived on March 27 and did not blow out until April 7. She would be classified as Storm-3 with sustained winds of 115 mph. But Phil and others in the convoy registered gusts close to 150 mph.

"We quickly lost sight of the other ships. We were pounded by 50-foot waves. PEONY's bow heaved up a mountainous wave, as her stern went underwater in the trough behind. When a wave rolled under the ship, it was like riding a surfboard." The ship would shudder like a dog with a chill.

Captain Eriksen had to keep PEONY's bow into the wind. If she turned broadside, the ship would be hit by the full force of wind and waves, broach and roll over. Phil found visibility from the bridge nearly zero.

At times PEONY was almost standing on her head. Every time her stern rose out of the water, the whole ship trembled and groaned, like a woman in childbirth, until the dampers slowed the spinning props.

"We took on so much water the crew had to abandon their quarters in the bow. Everyone was ordered topside, to stand watch in turn. Then the deck cargo, a load of 55-gallon drums of fuel oil, each weighing close to 600 pounds, broke loose and started careening across the deck. In the old days, cannons would break loose from their moorings and begin a wild ride below decks. Those loose cannons were almost impossible to capture, and could puncture the hull and sink a ship.

"It was the same with the weight and speed of these rogue oil drums. We had to render the barrels harmless. If one of these drums punched through a bulkhead of the officer's quarters, flooding them, it would make PEONY even more top heavy and almost impossible to steer."

Phil and a seaman named Bender climbed onto the main cargo hatch, putting them two feet above the deck, and went into action swinging fire-axes.

"We stayed out of the way of the rolling drums. Holding on to a safety line with one-hand, we spiked holes in the drums with our axes.

As the drums raced by, it was like trying to kill 600-pound cockroaches with a rolled-up newspaper. Each time we punctured a drum, it lost oil and was washed over the rails."

When all the loose drums were empty, Phil was confronted by another emergency. Seaman Kelly was missing. He hadn't shown up for his watch, and no one remembered seeing him.

"We started searching in the galley. The refrigerator had wrenched free and food was strewn everywhere. Their galley was a marsh of mashed-potatoes, gravy, meat loaf, cigarette butts, and vomit. Everyone was emptying his guts, sick from the storm and fear.

"As far as I could tell, Kelly was not in the galley. We hadn't checked the abandoned crew quarters in the forecastle. Getting there was really dodgy. I timed the waves right, and finally managed to reach the forecastle. But no Kelly.

"So I went back to the galley and began poking through the stinking swamp. There, hiding under the splinters of a galley table, Kelly was alive but catatonic, unable to move or call-out. Later I was relieved he was alive, but at the time I could've killed him."

The storm lasted 48 hours. All the lifeboats and rafts had been swept away. Everyone was puking, even Captain Eriksen. Phil had never been so frightened in his life. "I don't think any of us thought we'd survive."

Chapter 3 :

SIN CITY

Scrubbed clean of vomit and spilled fuel oil, PEONY arrived off China's great Yangtze River estuary at sunset, twenty days after leaving Manila, a voyage that would have taken only six days had convoy Captain Martin kept his libido under control. Sheer luck, and good seamanship by Captain Eriksen, had enabled them to survive Typhoon Barbara. They were to rendezvous with the rest of their five-ship convoy once they were safely upriver.

The vast mouth of the Yangtze is renowned for treacherous currents, shifting sandbars, and sunken hulks, as one of Asia's mightiest rivers sweeps roiling mud far out into the China Sea. The sky continued to be overcast, so even at midday Phil had not been able to determine their bearings with a sextant. Now darkness came quickly, obscuring landmarks, while the cloud layer made celestial navigation impossible.

Before fully entering the Yangtze, Phil somehow had to get PEONY's exact position, so he could chart a course. He did see a small island that he was able to identify on the charts. Using that island as a reference point, he laid a course to another island on the chart, from which he would plot a course for the last 48 miles up the delta to their rendezvous at the mouth of the smaller Whangpoo River entrance to Shanghai. But first he had to find the second island. Phil ordered seaman Bender to stand night-watch on the bow, to keep a sharp eye peeled for the island and not run run aground.

Hours passed, as PEONY nudged slowly through the gloom, then Phil began to hear the distinct sound of breakers on an approaching shore. In faint pre-dawn light, he could just make out the shape of the island he had been seeking. He altered course to steer parallel to the island. Annoyed that Bender had failed to warn him, Phil went forward stealthily to see why. He had a hunch that Bender was too busy hiding illicit goods from Chinese customs.

Prior to leaving Manila, PEONY's holds had been loaded with crates of consumer goods to stock U.S. Army post-exchanges in the Shanghai area: everything from cotton panties to peanut butter. As First Mate, Phil was responsible for the delivery of this expensive cargo. To his surprise, Bender, who had risked his life with Phil to gash holes in the rolling oil-drums, had appeared at Phil's cabin after the storm with the gift of a new bathrobe. On questioning, Bender admitted the bathrobe had come from that cargo, but would say no more. Phil guessed that another crewman had broken into the aft cargo-hold through the galley, and word of the PX goods had been too much of a temptation for most of the crew, including Bender. Brooding about it, Phil decided not to get mad, but to warn the crew that in Shanghai the cargo would be checked by U.S. Army officers against a manifest. So it would be difficult to explain missing items, and Phil would take the heat.

In the half-light as he went forward, he found crewmen skulking like rats, looking for places to hide their pilfered loot. Bender was on the bow as ordered, but instead of searching the horizon he was on his hands and knees, stashing his loot in an ammunition locker.

"Glad to see you're a praying man, Bender," Phil said off-handedly. "Be sure to let me know if you see the island." Startled, but still stuffing the locker, Bender answered without turning his head, "Yes sir". When Bender then got to his feet and saw the island a few hundred yards off the port side, he realized he had jeopardized the ship. Phil let it drop, and returned to the bridge to plot their new course upriver.

When PEONY arrived off the Whangpoo River, darkness had come again, bringing with it a dense fog. Captain Eriksen seemed to know intuitively where they were, and changed course, moving blind through the fog. Phil heard the mournful groans of fog-horns ahead, and what he thought might be the grunts of hard-working water buffaloes still plowing rice fields on an invisible shore. The ship slowed as Eriksen brought her to a dead halt.

He ordered the anchors down and reversed the engines for a moment to set the ship's two anchors in the muck. Only when the fog lifted the next morning did Phil realize what a navigational feat it Eriksen had achieved the night before. As the sun rose, he saw that PEONY was in the midst of a great armada of about a hundred ships. Big wooden junks called Scrambling Dragons mingled with ocean-going steel vessels of every size and type, while tiny three-plank sampans moved among them like water-bugs, rowed by single gaunt figures standing in the stern with a leg around one long sweep-oar. Eriksen's instincts and experience had guided PEONY to safety in near zero visibility. A Chinese Custom's vessel approached to check the ship and its papers.

Once cleared, a Chinese pilot took PEONY upstream 16 miles to the Shanghai Bund.

When the pilot brought PEONY alongside the U.S. Army wharf, the crew dropped mooring lines over huge bollards, and Phil braced for trouble. Not only was the convoy two weeks overdue, but their cargo was short because of pilfering. Four Army officers climbed out of an olive green sedan to take delivery. With relief, Phil learned that stocks at the PXs were so depleted, the officers were going to ignore formalities of the manifest and have their cargo off-loaded immediately. Soon cargo palettes were stacked high on the dock. Suddenly some empty boxes on the bottom collapsed under the weight of full boxes on top. Nobody batted an eye. Apparently pilfering was so commonplace here nobody was going to waste time arguing about a few empty crates. But Phil had one other worry.

In the after hold, hidden behind the PX cargo, was Phil's motorcycle, a 1940 Crocker Twin V, the big-tank model, which cruised happily at more than 100 mph. Once all the PX cargo was out of the hold, Phil went below to see if the Crocker had survived the typhoon. To his relief, his bike was not even scratched.

He had bought the Crocker in California before his first trip to Manila, leaving the bike with his family when he shipped out on LITTLE EVA. When next he was assigned to return to The Philippines on the ADMIRAL HUGHES, he decided to take the Crocker with him as contraband. He wanted to have some off-duty fun in The Philippines. Manila might be in ruins, but the rural countryside really was a paradise full of bamboo groves and flowering bougainvillea towering over thatch-roofed shacks. The bike would be contraband because valuable private property could not be shipped on any U.S. military vessel. At first he considered dismantling the bike and having friends smuggle it aboard in their duffles, piece-by-piece. That only spread the risk. So, typical of Phil, he decided to bluster his way and get the bike aboard 'legally'.

"The day before departure, I dressed in my best officer's uniform, got on the Crocker and rode down to the docks. The sailor standing guard at the pier entrance saluted and waved me past. So far, so good. At the wharf where the ADMIRAL HUGHES was being loaded, the officer in charge was a young ensign. I told him I was a passenger scheduled to leave on the HUGHES the next day. Naturally, I needed to take this bike. Falling for my guff, the ensign had the Crocker hoisted on deck, secured with rope, and covered with a tarp. He then got me transport back to base. It was that simple."

When PEONY was about to leave Cavite for Shanghai, Phil had stowed the Crocker in her hold before taking on the rest of her cargo, so he would have wheels in China. This time there was less anxiety because, as First Mate, the ship's cargo was his business. He convinced himself that in Shanghai such an exceptional bike could be sold for a handsome profit. Parts of China still controlled by the Nationalist government were shrinking faster than a cheap T-shirt. He had heard that Shanghai Chinese were packing up their noodle factories and escaping to Hong Kong or Taiwan. These days you could sell anything quickly in Shanghai if it was portable, especially if it could move fast. And, distracted as everybody was, the Army officers on the dock completely ignored his bike.

Shanghai was not to be confused with Shangri-La. As sin-cities go, Shanghai was at top of the list, a surprise for young Westerners like Phil who were new to Asia. For starters the Whangpoo, where PEONY was tied up, stank like an open sewer because it was an open sewer, and mortuary, for more than a million people. There was a nauseating smell of night-soil in the background everywhere, pungently seasoned with roasted garlic and the unbelievable wet-diaper stink of fish-paste, which could not be masked by anything, although people with cars tried to fend off the bad smell by hanging sprays of white jasmine flowers on their rear-view mirrors; but this jasmine smelled as bad as one of Captain Martin's bimbos.

When PEONY was unloaded, Captain Eriksen went on his usual binge ashore. Exactly where he went and what he drank, nobody knew. Night after night the blond giant was brought back to the dock in a rickshaw, passed out or close to it. Staggering out of the ricksha, he'd pull himself up the gangplank, gripping the ropes on either side, to collapse in his cabin bunk. At the end of the fifth straight night non-stop boozing, Eriksen was spotted by the Bosun on night-watch, towering over the perpetual crowd of Chinese on the Bund as he wove his way on rubbery legs to the side of the quay. As Eriksen groped blindly for the gangway ropes, he missed and fell straight into the Whangpoo, among orange peels, dead rats, and things you would rather not identify.

Another freighter was passing at that moment, its wake causing PEONY to sway toward the quay, and Phil saw that if Eriksen did not drown he would be crushed between the steel hull and the concrete. Phil yelled to the Bosun for a line, grabbed its bitter-end and jumped overboard. Fighting off thoughts of what he was plunging into, he caught Eriksen's sleeve, and gave the quayside a kick, propelling them both to the surface. As they broke the surface, Phil wrapped the line around Eriksen's chest under his arms, and gave it a hasty bosun's knot. A moment later both officers were hauled roughly onto the quay by crewmen.

Pausing only to shake off the foulness, Phil sloshed up the gangplank to the nearest showers, yelling for the crew to bring Eriksen. Stripping down while standing under a hot shower, shuddering with disgust, Phil told the crew to hold Eriksen under the next shower head.

The captain -- still unconscious -- spewed up his last pint of whatever. After dowsing him with fresh water, the crew dragged Eriksen none too gently to his cabin and dumped him on his bunk, leaving him in his soggy clothes. Next morning, Eriksen remembered nothing. He could not figure out why his clothes were wet and smelled so bad.

Originally the crew was to return to Manila immediately. But there were delays. Phil spent the time riding around Shanghai on his Crocker. There was a lot to do in the city, not all of it healthy. The U.S. Army made condoms available free, along with life's other essentials like beer and cigarettes.

A city guide, published for U.S. Army Air Corps personnel, gave particulars: "One of the most famous commodities that Shanghai has to sell is its night life. Thanks to the lavish spending of U.S. personnel this industry has snapped back to normal with a vengeance. ... Prophylactic items are available for personnel of this Headquarters at the dispensary in the Rockefeller Hospital Building. After 1700 hours prophylactic items will be available also at the MP stations of both the 14th Compound and the Rockefeller Compound." The notice ended: "Better than a pro - say no."

Phil had no interest in bars and brothels. He preferred to spend his free time making long excursions outside the city on the bike with his new pal, Chief Engineer Pete Peterson, who was good company. With Pete riding pillion, the two 21-year-olds toured the International Settlement, the French Quarter, the Chinese city, then crossed the iron bridge at Soochow Creek to see Hongkew. Stopping in a crowded, bar called The Gangplank, Pete gulped a warm beer, then turned to Phil: "This place is too damned dull."

He drew his Army issue Colt 45 automatic and, hardly bothering to aim, shot out every light in the bar while customers and the Chinese bartender dived for cover. Then Pete said: "Now this place is too damned dark, let's get out of here."

Pete was restless because his contract with the ATC was expiring. Each day he went hustling for a new job among the many foreign companies in buildings lining the Shanghai Bund, the Nanking Road, and their side streets. He was now accustomed to three square meals a day (even if this meant C-rations). Now he wanted a real roof over his head, clothes and a decent salary. He did not want to renew his contract with the ATC. He wanted to get on with life as a successful civilian. Here in bustling Shanghai he saw ways he could use his engineering credentials and military contacts to move into something better than the merchant marine.

He knew America was having problems adjusting to the economic downturn that peace brings after a long war. By contrast, Asia remained in conflict with civil war in China, and anti-colonial independence movements in the Dutch East Indies and elsewhere. In this superheated atmosphere, commercial enterprises continued to enjoy a bull-market. Peterson felt that if he took this moment to move into the private sector he could accumulate a far more substantial nest egg.

After canvassing job possibilities along the Bund, he knew he was right. By the fourth day Pete said he had found a honey of a job with good pay and expenses. He offered to get Phil a job at the same place, arguing that it was their karma to remain in Asia a while. As they discussed the future, 1946 looked like a promising year

Chapter 4 :

A PIECE OF CAKE

The opportunity Pete had discovered was with an outfit called JavaChina Trading Company at 17 Canton Road, a few meters off the Shanghai Bund, but with a clear view from the upstairs windows out over the Whangpoo. The job would be to supervise the reconditioning and delivery of surplus F-boats from Manila to private buyers in China, who were purchasing the ships through JavaChina. This was what Pete and Phil had just finished doing with the PEONY, for the U.S. Army Transport Corps. But doing this for JavaChina would pay a lot better than the wages they had received from the ATC. Plus, Pete raved, they would be civilians, and their own bosses. And JavaChina would also give them a generous per-diem to cover all their living expenses, in addition to the salary of $600 per month. They'd be able to live on the per diem and bank their wages. As civilians they would no longer be sleeping in a crowded Army quonset hut, and with the per diem they would not have to sleep on the ships. Life would be much better.

Though Shanghai was bursting with humanity, its labor market was starved for men with engineering skills and recent experience refitting surplus freighters.

While job-hunting, Peterson had prowled the tree-lined promenade of the Bund and stopped at the Long Bar for a beer, drawn for him by its famous Chinese bartender One-Long-Pour. Finding himself perched on a stool beside another young man, the two began to chat. Pete's drinking companion – Felix Hertzka – proved to be quite a talker.

After a perfunctory hand-shake and a few rounds, Pete learned a lot about Hertzka, sizing him up in the process. Hertzka was charming and agreeable, but also annoying and naive, liking to dramatize himself. He fit a certain mold: an overly handsome 25-year-old, a bit fey, who had fled Vienna in the 1930s to avoid Nazi persecution of Jews, ending up in Shanghai along with hundreds of thousands of other refugees. Technically a German citizen after Austria was absorbed by the Third Reich, Hertzka was not seen as an enemy by Axis Japan, so he had lived out the war in Shanghai as a free man, albeit watched closely and subjected to frequent interrogations by the Kempeitai. While Hertzka preened and prattled, his story was impressive. He was just back from Manila where he had concluded an agreement to purchase a number of decommissioned F-ships, a contract that promised to yield nearly $1,000,000 to his employer, JavaChina. Hertzka presented himself as the man in charge of the project. Now he had to find engineers and competent seamen to supervise the refitting and minor repairs to the ships, and who would see them safely to Shanghai.

When Pete said he'd just been part of such a ship delivery as an engineer for the ATC and that his Army contract was at its end, Hertzka's eyes widened. From the windows of JavaChina he had watched the brightly-painted PEONY arrive. Pete and his crew mates were just the sort Hertzka needed to bring this JavaChina venture to a successful conclusion, which might earn him a promotion to the company's new San Francisco office. Prodded by Pete, Hertzka explained proudly that he'd pulled off a brilliant deal in Manila.

Just a month earlier, in March, JavaChina had sent him to The Philippines to single-handedly negotiate the purchase of five surplus coastal cargo vessels from the U.S. authorities.

Hertzka boasted that he had been welcomed warmly to Manila by a U.S. Navy officer, a certain Commander Ennis. The two then entered into what Hertzka described as "hard-nosed negotiations" during which he "forced" Ennis to make numerous concessions to the demands of JavaChina. Hertzka said he had gotten everything he demanded. The price was $30,000 per ship, plus $7,000 each for refitting, to make them operational and seaworthy.

The extra charge of $7,000 per ship assured that all equipment removed in the mothball process would be restored and functional.

Commander Ennis gave Hertzka his word that the five ships would be ready to sail for Shanghai by the first week of June. From Hertzka's viewpoint, all that remained was to hire capable captains and crews to make the deliveries from Manila to Shanghai, before the June deadline to the Chinese buyers. Hertzka said the whole thing was "a piece of cake".

That evening Pete kicked it around with Phil, feeling bored and restless, up for anything that paid well. Phil agreed it would be a piece of cake.

The following morning, anxious to get his boss's approval, Hertzka took Pete and Phil to the JavaChina offices to meet the vice-president. Dr. Adolf Samet was an energetic 38-year-old Austrian refugee from the Nazis, who had a good grasp of economics, and managed JavaChina's daily operations.

As Hertzka had described him beforehand, Dr. Samet was like a three-minute egg, a bit hard outside, very soft inside, and a pushover for his own countrymen. After all, Samet had hired Hertzka on first acquaintance simply because he was a charming fellow Austrian, generously giving Hertzka the title Business Manager.

The excitable Samet was as short and round as a beer keg. But he had a paternal fondness for ambitious young men, so Pete and Phil fit naturally into Samet's hiring profile.

Like much of Shanghai's Bund, the offices of JavaChina had seen better days. But it did have an impressive view of the Whangpoo river if you craned your neck out the window.

Samet declared with utter confidence that the five F-boats would be handed over to JavaChina in Manila no later than the first week of June -- "in perfect running condition". Meantime, he explained how Chief Engineer Peterson and First Mate Mehan would serve as JavaChina's agents and 'supervisors' in Manila, to see that the ships were properly equipped and prepared for sea, as promised by Commander Ennis.

They would also be expected to hire crews on behalf of JavaChina, to help them deliver the ships to Shanghai.

Samet agreed that Pete and Phil would each be paid a salary of $600 a month, plus $300 a month to cover expenses and living accommodations, for a total of $900 in American currency -- a princely sum in 1946 for lads in their early twenties, especially in a part of the world where most things were dirt cheap. While Pete's ATC contract was indeed expiring, Phil said he was confident that he qualified to wind down his own ATC contract. So both men signed contracts with JavaChina that day.

On that occasion, neither met Samet's boss, Julius Winkelman, the Dutchman who was president and principal shareholder of JavaChina. They were told Winkelman was often on the road, arranging deals and financing to get the company back on its feet after the war. According to Hertzka, he was hard-nosed literally and physically, saber straight, with a dueling scar on his left cheek acquired while a student in The Netherlands before the war. Always in suit and tie, his hands fastidiously manicured, he could be blunt to the point of rudeness. His whole manner was arid and aloof. The only frivolous thing he had done in his life was to marry a stage performer.

JavaChina was only one of many foreign firms with offices on the Bund. It was founded long before the war by a group of Dutchmen in Java, who did import-export business throughout East Asia.

The Shanghai office had been owned jointly with local investors including some prosperous White Russian residents of the city's French Concession. During the war JavaChina was shut down and all its owners imprisoned. When Japan surrendered, the firm was dusted off, acquired and renovated by Winkelman, himself released only recently after four years in a Japanese prison camp in Shanghai. Winkelman was pouring family money into reviving JavaChina offices in different countries because his family had to face losing all their investments and land holdings in the Dutch East Indies, if the anti-colonial independence movement there was not put down harshly. If they had to leave Java, Winkelman and his brother and sister had no appetite for going back to The Netherlands, because their father had been the Dutch army chief-of-staff who surrendered Holland to the Nazis rather than see it destroyed. However good the general's motives, his action made many enemies.

Winkelman was an expert trader, deft at arranging deals to buy, sell, and deliver goods. From time to time he leased ships to expedite cargoes for his clients. This gave him only a basic familiarity with ship-brokerage, not a profound knowledge of what really makes ships seaworthy. Yet he was feverishly ambitious, inclined to make assumptions and take chances. It was Winkelman who had been excited to hear that the United States was selling cheap surplus cargo ships and other vessels through America's War Damage Commission in Manila. So he had authorized Samet to send Hertzka to Manila to purchase some.

The many risks involved in buying and selling used ships also were not something Winkelman fully understood.

But he wanted to make a fortune before Mao took power in China. He was already setting up fall-back offices in San Francisco and New York, if he had to flee Shanghai as well as Java. He admired America, and was more confident than he should have been that doing business with U.S. colonial authorities in Manila would be trouble free. He saw a chance for big profits buying vessels as an intermediary for wealthy Shanghai clients, especially as panic grew over the outcome of China's civil war. There was an urgent demand from Shanghai entrepreneurs for small cargo ships that could carry weapons upriver, or flight-cargo down the coast. China's interior was now largely in the hands of the Reds, so the civil war was becoming more of a coastal affair. Nationalists still controlled port cities along the coast, and inland ports on the Yangtze's south bank. These were often very shallow waters, with shifting sandbars and mudbanks, so the smaller freighters called F-boats seemed perfect. Timing was crucial as thousands of Chinese merchants were frantic to get their cotton mills and noodle factories relocated to British Hong Kong or Taiwan before Shanghai fell to the Communists.

JavaChina was only acting as a broker, buying the F-boats for its Chinese customers, who were putting up all the money, and paying a hefty mark-up.

The clients would be paying $121,000 for each vessel on delivery in Shanghai giving JavaChina a profit of $90,000 x 5 ships. The Chinese were not exactly being reamed, for at that time small ships like these could earn around $80,000 a month, providing they were in fair condition.

According to the contract approved by Hertzka in Manila, the F-boats would be handed over to JavaChina's representatives in Manila no later than the first week of June 1946 -- only two months away -- "in perfect running condition".

Meantime, Chief Engineer Peterson and First Mate Mehan would serve as JavaChina's 'supervisors' and representatives in Manila to oversee all work, and find crews. Hertzka and Dr. Samet seemed hugely relieved to have Pete and Phil take on this huge responsibility, removing the burden from their shoulders.

Dazzled by their good fortune, Phil decided then and there to sell his Crocker motorcycle. Anyone with eyes could see the Nationalist economy was collapsing. Inflation was out of control. Everyone in Shanghai was unloading laundry baskets of Nationalist currency to acquire dollars or other hard assets that were portable. The Crocker fit the bill, although Phil was grieved to see that Chinese did not really appreciate its unique qualities; they only knew the Harley-Davidson brand. A black market deal was concluded, and Phil parted company with the Crocker for $550. He consoled himself that he would make serious money delivering the ships to JavaChina.

Indeed, the future did look sunny, but Pete and Phil were in for a surprise. Storm clouds were gathering, worse than any typhoon. The old nautical grind goes: Red sky at night, sailors delight. Red sky in the morning, sailors take warning. It would be a red sky in the morning.

Chapter 5 :

RED DAWN

In appearance, a 'balut' looks like a normal boiled egg that English nannies serve with fingers of toast to their upper-class charges. In reality, a balut is a fertilized duck or chicken egg that is incubated for some seventeen days. When the egg is candled and reveals a chick inside, although without yet having developed feathers or a beak, it is dropped into boiling water and soft-cooked or hard-cooked according to a customer's wishes. Filipinos often consume a dozen balut at a sitting -- shell and tissue -- pausing only to dip the delicacy into a salt and vinegar sauce, then wash it down with ice-cold beer. Sometimes a balut is served as a joke to foreign tourists in Manila to shock them. It serves as a symbol of nasty surprises waiting, once you get past the familiar shell of The Philippines and bite into what's really inside.

When Phil and Pete signed on with JavaChina in April 1946, they knew little of the realities of life in The Philippines, except that the islands were beautiful, as were many of the women. Everybody knew the place had been ruled in turn by Chinese pirates, Spaniards, Americans, and Japanese, most Filipinos were desperately poor, and power was in the hands of a small group of rich oligarch families, who were in bed with American generals and Washington politicians. It seemed that simple.

Less than seven months after the surrender of Japan, the obsessively Catholic Philippines were warned of a new Satan: the Red Beast of communism. Today most people think the Cold War began with the Berlin Airlift or the Korean War. In Asia it actually began in the Philippines early in 1946 when an authentic land reform movement of poor farmers known as the Huks was mischievously re-labeled as a deadly Marxist conspiracy to overthrow the government. By wildly exaggerating its size and potential, claiming it was being funded and supplied by Moscow, pouring gasoline on the rural fire, it was made to seem like a raging civil war, requiring urgent attention and millions of dollars in military aid to Manila. The man who went out of his way to provoke this, and then polished his skills in Vietnam, Laos, and Cambodia, was the former advertising agency copywriter Edward Lansdale. He had spent World War II in San Francisco writing propaganda for the OSS, then was sent to Manila in 1945 to keep him on the payroll under the escutcheon of U.S. Army Counter-Intelligence, G-2. Lansdale did not dream up the Cold War, but he was an agent of those who did. His corporate clients this time were a powerful group of conservative American bankers, lawyers, bureaucrats, and journalists in Wall Street and Washington known collectively as The Georgetown Set. More on them later in our story.

The war with Japan twice altered political relationships throughout Asia. In China, the Dutch East Indies, Malaya, Indochina, Burma, and The Philippines, resistance groups fighting the Japanese became America's allies. When the war ended, the same guerrilla forces became America's enemies, without exception. In most cases the guerrillas continued to fight for independence from returning colonial powers, British, French, or Dutch.

During Japan's occupation of The Philippines, there were guerrilla bands on different islands, but the most effective fighters were the Huks of central Luzon. Some 50,000 men and women, mostly tenant farmers in Pampanga and neighboring provinces, they took to the hills and harassed the Japanese effectively, often aided by American soldiers who escaped during the Bataan Death March. Most Huks had no education or political ideology, and were driven to rebellion by the tyranny of big landowners. But among their leaders were a few student activists who entered politics after the war to continue campaigning for land reform. The big landowners fought back by calling them Marxist radicals and terrorists. Their voices were heard in Washington where conservatives were regaining power following the death of President Roosevelt. A global sea-change was underway that would again make fascism fashionable, while demonizing America's erstwhile allies, and anyone who sympathized with them would be the targets of witch-hunters, like Senator McCarthy. With things going badly in China for the U.S. backed regime of Chiang Kai-shek, the prospect of imminent communist victory there electrified the Pentagon, White House and State Department, where the New Right carried out pogroms of leftists, liberals, and progressives.

In February 1946, the U.S. Congress debated the issue of Huk veteran rights. It had long been established that any Filipino who served the U.S. military, including those who fought as guerrilla against the

Japanese, were to be considered as American soldiers. In a move that shocked Filipinos, Congress initially denied the Huks their rights and benefits under the GI Bill, breaking a promise made to them by General MacArthur. They were also denied back-pay, hospitalization, mustering-out pay, and burial benefits. It was the first legislative sign that America had now entered into a Cold War mentality, not against a particular nation but against an alien state of mind, colored red, subgroup terrorist.

Philippine independence remained on schedule for July 4, 1946. The election for positions in the new government was held in April. The handsome and popular young Huk leader Luis Taruc easily won a seat in congress but he and other Huk candidates were then rejected on unspecific allegations of 'voting irregularities'. Shunned by the ruling elite, the Huks retreated into the rainforest and mountains they knew so well, and resumed their insurrection. The newly elected President Manuel Roxas, MacArthur's designated candidate, declared a "mailed fist" policy toward the Huks. The mailed fist was Major Lansdale at U.S. Army G-2 in Manila.

Lansdale's solution to the Huk 'problem' was a campaign of terror. As psychological warfare, he had village walls painted with the 'all-seeing-eye' of the ancient Egyptian sun god, called the Eye-of-Ra, then had villagers march in single file past a hooded figure whose nod was a death sentence -- a tactic borrowed from the Japanese.

With an unlimited budget, Lansdale created death squads called Nenita Units, whose mission was to find and kill Huks wherever they could be found, including men, women, and children -- a policy the CIA later called 'gradual extermination'. When armed Huks proved strangely difficult to find, all effort was devoted to wiping out villages 'assumed' to be associated somehow with the Huks. Hundreds of villages across central Luzon were mortared, shelled, torched with flame-throwers. American napalm was used to destroy crops and villages. Those farmers who escaped the flames were rounded up and shot. This brutality, worse than that of the Japanese occupation, later became notorious in Vietnam. Stripped of ornamentation, it was a policy to eliminate all Filipino peasant farmers who would not submit to the ruthless exploitation of the local oligarchic families favored by Washington.

As Lansdale had zero combat experience, he sought out American veterans with unusual experience killing Japanese hand-to-hand.

Foremost among them was Lieutenant Charles 'Boh' Bohannan, who had made a name for himself during the war killing Japanese singlehandedly in New Guinea. To head all the Nenita death squads Lansdale and Bohannan chose a sleekly handsome Filipino with a bottomless appetite for killing.

Napoleon Valeriano was a graduate of the Philippine Military Academy who had fought in Bataan, then escaped from a Japanese prison camp to be picked up by a U.S. submarine and taken to Australia. There he became a protege of MacArthur and his head of G-2, General Charles Willoughby, with whom Valeriano shared a pathological anti-communism. Valeriano rose to colonel's rank in the U.S. Army, and after Japan's surrender went after the men he blamed for his father's death during the war, whom he believed to be members of 'the Manila Politburo'. It was the start of his new career dedicated to anticommunist death squads and 'skull-squadrons' in The Philippines, Indochina, and Central America, all under the guidance of Lansdale and Bohannan.

In Luzon, they applied these terror tactics to everyone they could find in large tracts of land considered 'free kill zones' in which death squads killed all villagers, farmers, loggers, fishermen, rural laborers, or members of isolated tribes of aborigines. No effort was made to identify them as Huks before they were killed.

The reason Lansdale had such a deep purse and a completely free hand to say and do whatever he wished, was an event that happened in total secrecy, making him the darling of what would become the new CIA. Immediately after his first arrival in Manila in September 1945, Lansdale heard the buzz in G-2 about a secret operation at Bilibad Prison where a Filipino agent named Santa Romana was torturing a Japanese officer. The prisoner, Major Kojima Kashii, had driven General Yamashita around in a command car during the last months of the war. It was widely believed that Kojima knew the locations of secret vaults where the Japanese had hidden tons of treasure taken as war loot from across Asia. In previous months, big hoards of Nazi gold and art treasures had been found in Europe. The Japanese hoard could be even bigger, as Japan had started looting many years earlier when it invaded Korea in 1895. If Santa Romana could force Kojima to show them the vaults, America could recover vast sums of gold, platinum, barrels of currency taken from banks, and priceless art works including solid gold

Buddha statues. Even better, The Philippines were still an American colony, so there would be no need to share the treasure with the allies, as had happened in Europe.

Excited, Lansdale put himself in charge of the torture. Eventually he persuaded Santa Romana to try bribery, and soon afterward Major Kojima showed them the entrances to twelve vaults scattered across northern Luzon. Inside they found solid gold ingots stacked six feet tall in row after row across chambers the size of tennis courts. Lansdale flew to Tokyo to brief MacArthur, then to Washington where he briefed the War Department and President Truman's chief security adviser, Navy Commander Clark Clifford. Truman decided the vaults in The Philippines must be recovered secretly to avoid a global financial crisis.

While Lansdale was in Washington, Clifford introduced him to an inner circle of The Georgetown Set, a group of influential journalists, politicians and government officials and their socialite wives, who gathered at their town houses each week to discuss and often manipulate politics. Best known among them in the late 1940s were policy-makers such as Averill Harriman, John McCloy, Paul Nitze, George Kennan, Dean Acheson, David Bruce, Walt Rostow, and 'Chip' Bohlen -- essentially pointmen for the most powerful families in America. The hard core of The Georgetown Set were a small group of secretive and conspiratorial men who would head the new CIA: Allen Dulles, and Richard Bissell, Tom Braden, Cord Meyer, James Angleton, Tracy Barnes, Frank Wisner, and Desmond FitzGerald. Because Allen Dulles knew little about the Orient, Wisner and FitzGerald would be in charge of black operations in Asia. This group adopted Lansdale, and for years afterward whenever he was in Washington, he was a favorite guest at the weekly drinking parties in the Dulles household. There he became especially close to Wisner and FitzGerald. As a man obsessed by secret societies and covert operations, Lansdale had fantasies of cabals ruling Europe and the United States from the shadows. His introduction to the Dulles coven, and its extreme secrecy, affirmed his most eccentric imaginings. These men imagined themselves to be the Eye-of-Ra, the all-seeing sun-god, at the top of the human pyramid, whose responsibility was to maintain surveillance and control of everyone beneath them. Indeed, in the 18th century, Freemasons had been famously involved in revolutionary movements in Europe. Some of America's Founding Fathers were Masons. Among them were Ben Franklin George Washington, Thomas Jefferson, Benedict Arnold, Samuel Adams, and John Hancock. The pervasive influence of Freemasonry was manifest for all to see in the cryptic symbols on U.S. Currency, the Great Seal, and the designs and inscriptions of monuments and public buildings in the capital. From this it was only a small jump to Lansdale's fetish with the Eye-of-Ra, the magisterial eye of the ruling Establishment, and its self-proclaimed illuminati.

Flattered and inspired by all the attention, Lansdale returned to Manila with a free hand to do whatever he could to block the spread of communism in Asia, starting with the Huks.

By the time Pete and Phil returned to Manila to work on the surplus freighters for JavaChina, Lansdale was counting the ears cut off dead Huks by Napoleon Valeriano, and downing stiff cocktails at the bar in the Manila Hotel. Soon, the unsuspecting young men would be added to Lansdale's list of "Huk collaborators" and "dangerous communist suspects".

Chapter 6 :

BUYER BEWARE

They returned to Manila from Shanghai on the ATC transport SS JOHN MCLEAN. The voyage was uneventful, the only nuisance a case of small-pox among the MCLEAN's crew, so when they reached Manila passengers and crew had to spend three extra days in shipboard quarantine.

Once cleared by health authorities, Pete and Phil returned to ATC quarters at Camp Two: some aging Quonset huts laid out on a grid plan that the sun turned into a bread-oven that April. When monsoon season began shortly, the quonset huts would become cold, damp and miserable. There was constant bickering, horseplay, fighting and bullying among the officers awaiting reassignment. Having sold the Crocker, they had no easy escape.

Peterson easily terminated his contract with the ATC, but Phil had problems. Every officer he spoke to brushed him off, refusing to be specific, putting him at risk legally by having two employers, JavaChina and the Army Transport Corps. His ATC contract had been for the duration of the war plus six months. Six months after Japan's surrender had fallen in March. However, the ATC was losing officers and crew as nearly everyone was anxious to go home, and get on with life. Men who had served a long time overseas, and had wives and children waiting for them, had preference. To his dismay, Phil was suddenly promoted to captain and assigned to take command of a small freighter bound for Leyte. Under different circumstances, a promotion, pay rise, and ship command would have been very welcome. But this promotion put him in a different category for discharge. It was time to pull another rabbit out of the hat.

In the military, a direct approach was doomed, unless you took people off guard, so he tried the most radical approach possible -- telling the truth. Seeking out the highest ranking ATC official in Manila, he confessed that he had made a commitment to JavaChina in Shanghai because he assumed his ATC contract had expired. Startled that somebody should be so honest, the official was reasonable. He demoted Phil from Captain to his old rank of First Mate. The ATC was short of captains, but had an abundance of first mates. So Phil could now obtain an immediate discharge. On May 13, 1946, he was mustered out of the ATC.

In less than one month, the five F-boats were due to be turned over formally to JavaChina in Manila, and it would then be up to Phil and Pete to deliver them to Shanghai.

Their fantasies of an easy life vaporized when the two pals made their first trip south around Manila Bay to Cavite, to inspect the ships Felix Hertzka had purchased sight-unseen.

Instead of seaworthy vessels needing minor cosmetic repairs, they saw rust-buckets, cannibalized from bridge to keel. Diesel engines, generators, boilers, and tools were gone. The galley had been picked clean of every pot, knife, fork and spoon. Crew quarters were stripped of bedding. The radio shack was gutted. The bridge lacked even a compass or intercom. What was still on board seemed beyond repair.

Hertzka had been bamboozled.

Years later, when Samet was a sadder and wiser man, he clarified what had happened: "To put the matter in a nutshell ... Hertzka arranged with the man in charge of the sales in Manila, Commander Ennis, that the ships would be repaired and put in perfect running condition by the U.S. Army before being delivered to JavaChina. ... including wireless sending and receiving set, and stores, as well as spare parts. ... especially that the ships will be ready for delivery in Manila latest first week June 1946. On this basis the purchase was concluded and JavaChina paid total purchase price to the U.S. Army Finance Officer in Shanghai. When the contracts were returned to JavaChina signed by the Foreign Liquidation Commission in Manila, we found that all the points, specified above, ... were not mentioned in the contract."

Making matters worse, JavaChina had strict contract obligations of its own to get these ships to powerful Chinese buyers by the end of June. These contracts included severe penalty fees if delivery was delayed, or the ships were not properly seaworthy.

Ultimately, Phil was forced to conclude that JavaChina's boss had been out of his depth buying used ships, and Felix Hertzka had only been the most obvious part of the mess.

"Their primary business had been import-export, which Winkelman knew through and through, but by the time this was all over, he rued the day he deviated from what he knew best and got involved in purchasing these boats."

True, the five ships purchased for JavaChina had not been chosen by Hertzka, they had been chosen by Commander Ennis, who selected the dregs of the mothballed fleet, to get rid of the worst of the worst. This was a question of quality, not size. In size they fit the bill. About half the length of PEONY, these mini-freighters were only 100 feet long, with a draft of 10 feet, ideal for Chinese coastal and riverine trade, where they could enter all but the smallest harbors.

But if their poor condition kept them from being delivered to Shanghai within a reasonable grace period after the June deadline, it could bankrupt JavaChina, and Julius Winkelman, who doubtless would put the blame on Pete and Phil.

Like the children's game 'Gossip', Hertzka had listened to Ennis, Samet listened to Hertzka, Winkelman listened to Samet, Phil and Pete listened to Hertzka, Samet, and Winkelman. A lot was lost in translation. The devil was in the details.

As they looked over the five vessels, it did not seem likely that any of them could be made ready to go by early June – barely three weeks away.

Commander Ennis was no longer there to blame. He was half way across the Pacific, returning to a very comfortable civilian life in America.

Disappointed, Pete and Phil consoled themselves that they had a lush contract with JavaChina. So they set out to do whatever necessary -- on and off the books -- to make the boats seaworthy enough for the trip, even if some refitting had to be completed in China. A year earlier, they might have wheedled cooperation out of Army dockworkers. But having resigned from the ATC, neither could expect brotherly sympathy. They would have to use money instead. By the spring of 1946, the Army was drastically reducing its repair and maintenance operations in The Philippines. The Cavite shipyard was notoriously lethargic. Its commissioned and non-commissioned officers were daydreaming about getting home. Given a bribe, officers at Cavite might promise to cooperate, but all requests still had to go through bureaucratic red-tape at the Foreign Liquidation Commission. Those elbows would also need grease.

Even when they were authorized to pick up equipment from Army depots, they found the warehouses empty. In Manila, things vanished as in the Bermuda Triangle. Much of this disappearing was arranged by officers who sold Army property, surplus or not, to gangsters on the black market. Army investigations noted: "A Commander Bean is reported to have banked $25,000 more than he could possibly have saved from his salary during the time he worked for the Foreign Liquidation Commission."

Bean's $25,000 was small potatoes during postwar reconstruction. Civilian carpetbaggers made fortunes from the misfortunes of others. Small fish helped themselves to cigarettes and booze, while more accomplished thieves worked with pocket armies in wholesale lots. Four months after the liberation of Manila, over $1-million in U.S. government-owned goods were 'recovered by police' from a warehouse owned by enemies of Elpidio Quirino. This was good publicity for a vice-president famous for corruption. In fact, the police were sent to the warehouse by Quirino's brother Tony 'The Fixer'. The goods had first been hijacked by Quirino's Ilocano mafia, which kept the best items, then dumped the rest as 'evidence' to embarrass rivals.

One of the Quirinos' associates was notorious ex-GI Harry Stonehill. Together they reaped millions from gambling, black market and trade monopolies. Harry had arrived in Manila as a young lieutenant in 1945, working like Commander Bean and Commander Ennis in the Foreign Liquidation Commission. On the side he sold surplus Army trucks to the underworld. After his discharge, he dumped his plain-Jane wife in the States, returned to Manila as a partner of young Ilocano upstart Ferdinand Marcos, and worked his way up the food-chain to the Quirino brothers.

While Elpidio Quirino was boss, day to day operations were overseen by his middle brother, Judge Antonio Quirino, or Tony 'The Fixer'. Since the 1930s, they had been close to General MacArthur and his inner circle of attorneys, investment advisers, and U.S. Army aides. All MacArthur's men were aware that the Quirino Machine got 5% to 10% of every government transaction, aside from what they hijacked, or collected in kickbacks. In exchange, the Ilocano underworld provided muscle for law enforcement, and kept MacArthur's aides apprised of dangerous political tendencies in the islands. This effectively gave the

Quirinos a hammerlock on government, the courts, and the black market. Although, for the time being, they were prepared to let someone else, like Quezon, take the bows as president.

Unable to meet the Quirinos' black market prices, Phil and Pete turned for help to lesser hustlers. They also started bribing U.S. Army officers at Cavite with $100 bills, to move things forward.

"We had to grease Army palms to get it done. Worse than that, once you made a deal with one officer and paid him off, he would be transferred, so you had to slip another hundred, and another and another."

Informed of these obstacles, and the poor condition of the five mini-freighters, JavaChina strangely decided to buy two more F-boats that were in far better condition, apparently on the assumption that they might be made seaworthy sooner. However, even these two newer ships would never make the end of June deadline in Shanghai.

With daily bribery and dogged tenacity, by June 3, 1946, Phil and Pete had accomplished miracles. Holding out a carrot, the U.S. Army did promise to expedite delivery of the two newer ships. Phil was annoyed by this thimblerigging, but he felt personally responsible: "It's absolutely imperative that I deliver these two ships to China before July 1st, or JavaChina will lose thousands of dollars."

Barring a typhoon, the voyage to Shanghai would take only seven days. So the deadline for departure would have to be June 24, two weeks away.

On June 13, a tall, fair-haired man in his late twenties picked his way through the shipyard debris. He was neatly dressed but the day was like a sauna, so his pressed shirt and slacks were stained with sweat. Speaking good English with what sounded like a Russian accent, he introduced himself as Vadim Chirskoff -- "Just call me Cheez".

In response to all their anxious messages, JavaChina had sent Cheez from Shanghai to help them expedite the repairs and deliveries. As money was the only way to grease the process, he came as a bagman with fat rolls of U.S. dollars.

When they saw how full Cheez's pockets were, they thought their problems were solved. But be careful what you wish for.

They knew nothing about Cheez. Nor was Cheez in the habit of explaining himself, especially now that he hoped to turn over a new leaf and be seen as an upwardly mobile young international businessman. This was a one-in-a-million chance to start life over, and rescue his family from the growing chaos in China.

His life had been so different from Phil or Pete that he could have come from another galaxy. Born in 1917 in Vladivostok, Siberia, he was the son of White Russian emigres, apolitical intellectuals from St. Petersburg who had fled east to escape the communist revolution and subsequent Bolshevik Terror. Cheez did not expect these two Americans to know the difference between White Russians and Red Russians. Whether Russians favored the Czar, or favored replacing him with democracy, or even the creation of a Marxist paradise, most Russians did favor staying alive. Those opposed to the Bolsheviks, or who simply wished to survive, were lumped together as White Russians, and the prudent among them fled wherever they could. Those who stayed to fight the Red Russians died in huge numbers.

In Siberia, Cheez's mother suffered terribly from arthritis, so when he was just turning eight years old they fled on to Japan where she had treatment at a resort with hot sulphur springs. When she felt better, they moved on to Yokohama, south of Tokyo. At age ten, Cheez entered the fourth year of elementary school at St. Joseph's College there, graduating in 1934 with a highschool diploma. He found a temporary job in a lawyer's office, then a better one at the Tokyo office of the Hollywood movie company United Artists, and finally what could become a permanent job at a Swiss import-export firm named Lichman-Waelchl Company. Despite his youth, he was constantly hounded and interrogated by Japanese police, who considered him a Communist just because he was of Russian birth. Everywhere in the world in those days, even White Russians were Reds. Rattled by the harassment, Cheez found a berth as a seaman on a Swedish ship, crossed the Pacific, and spent several years in and out of ports North and South America. Worried about his aging parents, he returned to Yokohama in 1939 to find Japan in a frenzy of war-fever, as the Imperial Army struck south through China and carried out the gruesome Rape of Nanking, where over 60,000 women and girls were gang-raped, and some 210,000 Chinese massacred. If what he learned from his parents about the Bolshevik Terror in Russia was horrific, the inhumanity of the Japanese Terror was now confirmed as well.

Shanghai had come under Japanese control, but remained outwardly an open international city, a place where you could make a fast buck if you did not get your throat slit. Unlike Phil and Pete, who often talked longingly of going home, Cheez did not come from any place he wanted to go back to. He left Japan for China in 1939, then sent for his parents, supporting them by working as a salesman for a shipyard building barges, ships, and tugboats.

He married a pretty White Russian emigre in Shanghai, Nina Denisova, whose parents had been investors in JavaChina before the war. Nina bore him a son they named Georgyi or Georgie. There were a great many Russian refugees in Shanghai. After Pearl Harbor they were not interned by the Japanese because the Soviet Union was at war with Nazi Germany, not with Japan.

"We existed on money I made from odd jobs or occasional sales of black market articles among foreign traders dealing in needles, milk, U.S. dollars, and so forth.

'After the war, I was able to secure U.S. Army food contracts and, thanks to these, I worked with JavaChina, supplying the U.S. Army Transportation Command with meat, vegetables, eggs, and other articles." He also continued working in the shipyard, rebuilding damaged barges and ships, and repairing motorcycles on the side. In all these jobs, Cheez naturally mingled with other Russian emigres who spoke his language, were in similar predicaments, and helped each other when they could. At 28, Cheez was not that much older than Pete or Phil. But his experience of desperate survival, and the hustling required, was light-years beyond the brash young Americans. Like all Russians who seem to have come from a dark novel by Dostoevsky, he masked his misery with poetic fatalism. He might be a man without roots, but he was not a man without hope. After a few drinks he became gregarious, loud, boisterous, and raunchy. Russians never sipped vodka, they tossed it down then bit into a pickled onion to kill the taste. They approached life the same way.

So it was that another foreign exotic entered the story from stage left, this one towing a barge of tragedy but also thousands of dollars of company assets earmarked for their salaries and living expenses, for crew salaries, for bribes, plus enough extra to buy several cheap surplus landing craft and PT-boats. Winkelman had told Cheez that he -- Winkelman -- might consider setting up a business in The Philippines, using PT-boats or landing craft to haul frozen fish, lumber or grated coconut (copra).

Cheez planned to find just such an opportunity. He was not evil, or malignant, nor was he in a hurry to deposit the company funds. He was exhilarated by Manila, the lavish wages, the liberty, and his first chance to enjoy the life of a successful businessman in a tropical paradise. In this he, and Phil and Pete, had enough in common to make their new arrangement click.

Chapter 7 :

SCENE OF THE CRIME

When Cheez left them at Cavite, he invited Pete and Phil to be his guests for dinner at 10 o'clock that evening in the Manila Hotel, the favorite watering hole of wealthy Americans and Filipinos, both the savory and the unsavory. From the bankroll Cheez kept waving around, he could afford the best. They returned to their temporary accommodations in a low-rent district of Manila to shower and change. Pete even shaved off his sideburns, which had grown into Victorian muttonchops. Scrubbed of grit and grease, and wearing clean shirts and slacks, they ambled into the Manila Hotel a few minutes early. Their eyes widened at the vast open spaces and sheer elegance. They'd never seen anything like it, and felt completely out of place. They tried to look casual but felt like grease-monkeys.

The hotel's regular clients were only beginning to arrive in dark sedans, men in dinner jackets or embroidered Barongs, women in long dresses or Filipino gowns with puffed shoulders called Ternos. Spotting Cheez across the wide dining room, they picked their way through round or square tables set for four, dodging beautiful girls and fish-eyed mothers.

Cheez, dressed as though he belonged there in dark slacks and an embroidered Barong-Tagalog, stood up to greet them. Penguin-suited waiters pulled out chairs. The tables were spaced so diners could talk in private, while keeping an eye on everyone else. Chandeliers lit the high ceilings, while each table had shaded lamps to cast softer glows on the more wrinkled dowagers. Cheez seemed to know how to use slight gestures to bring waiters running. He ordered appetizers, entrees, salads, plus what he said was a very good claret. When a waiter corrected Pete for using the wrong fork, Cheez raised an eyebrow as if to ask what was impeccable food without impeccable waiters.

In 1946 this was the only fashionable address in The Philippines, a masterpiece of social architecture consolidating four and a half centuries of arrogant colonialism. During the Spanish-American War, large parts of Spanish Manila had been destroyed, then rebuilt in what was called 'the American vision'. Beside Manila Bay, Architect William Parsons was given the job of designing a world-class hotel to rival the Spaniards' Malacañang Palace on the Pasig River.

The building Parsons designed was appropriately in Spanish Colonial style, white with a green roof, shaped like an H, set in 3.5 hectares of verdant gardens at the head of palm-lined Taft Boulevard. Most impressive were its cool, high-ceilinged interior spaces, all white with carved Philippine-mahogany accents. In what at the time was a vast lobby, 125-feet long by 25-feet wide, the white marble floor was lined with Doric columns, potted palms, clusters of oversized couches and lounge chairs where the elite could gossip and bargain. On the roof terrace were gardens with an unimpeded view of sunsets over Bataan Peninsula. This roof terrace proved convenient in 1935 when The Philippines achieved semi-independent status, and President Manuel Quezon asked General Douglas MacArthur to create a Philippine Army. As MacArthur's father was one of the Yankee generals who had exterminated one million Filipino 'goo-goos', Douglas MacArthur had spent his childhood in Manila, serving as his father's aide. Like his father, he became an intimate of Manila's powerful oligarchs. Thanks to the path prepared for him, Douglas MacArthur had risen to become U.S. Army Chief of Staff under President Herbert Hoover, only to be removed from that post by incoming President Franklin Roosevelt. FDR detested MacArthur for his arrogance, incompetence, and presidential ambitions, and wanted to get him far away from Washington. At this crucial moment when MacArthur's career might have ended, President Quezon stepped into the breech with his request that MacArthur be assigned to create a national army for The Philippines. This gave FDR an easy way to post the general to the other side of the planet.

Quezon had known MacArthur since boyhood, and understood that if the general could not live in Malacañang Palace, the seat of the governor-general, some other place of similar majesty must be created. So Quezon built a palatial penthouse atop the Manila Hotel. The hotel, owned by the Philippine government, was conveniently across a park from the Army and Navy Club, MacArthur's favorite haunt.

Quezon wrote off the cost of the penthouse and covered its monthly rent of $1,500 by selling the hotel to a group of cronies and naming MacArthur chairman of the Manila Hotel Corporation. Public and private interests were like gin-and-tonic.

The MacArthur penthouse had a mahogany-paneled dining room, a library with 8,000 books inherited from his father, a spacious parlor, and a grand kitchen. MacArthur never cooked, and only had to tell the hotel kitchen when he wanted his favorite food, the large fish called grouper. MacArthur liked his Lapu-Lapu steamed and served in banana leaves. Frequent guests in the penthouse were MacArthur's circle of business tycoons, investment bankers, and attorneys.

During the Japanese occupation, the penthouse was taken over by Japan's Prince Chichibu, eldest of Emperor Hirohito's three brothers. The hotel remained undamaged at war's end because pilots had strict orders to avoid targeting it, or Malacañang Palace, or the city's ancient cathedrals. After Japan's surrender, MacArthur gave the privilege of restoring and managing the hotel to a man he trusted absolutely, the late President Quezon's confidential aide and intelligence chief, Colonel Manuel Nieto. His new post was in the nature of a secret service assignment, for Nieto did not need a job. He was a millionaire in his own right, with tobacco plantations in the Ilocos, and a confidante of the Quirino brothers. The hotel had always been a place of assignations, and Nieto's real job was to keep an eye on everything happening, a way for MacArthur to monitor Congressional delegations from Washington and VIP visitors from other countries. Many guest rooms had their phones rigged for monitoring private conversations. Bellhops and roomboys were coached in what to look for, desk clerks were trained by G-2 to record calls, steam open letters, and copy radiograms.

Journalist John Gunther said at the time that Nieto was "a fine athlete and boxer" who "knows all the secrets". Nieto had been in the small group who escaped with MacArthur from Corregidor. Now he also held key posts in the War Reconstruction Administration, the biggest pork barrel in Philippine history. This combination of wealth, power, skill with guns and fists, and connections to palace, underworld and G-2, made Nieto a dangerous adversary.

That first evening, over their dinner at the Manila Hotel, Cheez said Pete and Phil were to move into the hotel, where they would have rooms in a grand suite Cheez had reserved. As official expediter for JavaChina, Cheez would use company money to cover all their hotel expenses. They would be dealing with top American and Filipino

49

bureaucrats, officers, or business people, so they had to look smart and have an impressive address. Neither Phil nor Pete raised any objections, although Pete resisted moving in right away. He had found a cheap apartment that he now shared with his girl friend Connie. It was a ground floor apartment with an attached garage. Phil had moved in with them temporarily, sleeping on the couch in the living room. It saved him rent, but he was not at all happy witnessing the rough-and-tumble romance between Pete and Connie. In private, Pete was domineering, keeping Connie on a tight leash. She never knew what to expect when he came home: Snuggles, beatings, or both in rapid succession. One day Pete brought a bouquet of flowers, next day he would throw a bouquet in her face. If something bad happened at Cavite, he took his rage out on her. Like many young Filipinas, Connie was pretty, but had no money and no safety net. Her education had been interrupted by the Japanese occupation. No self-respecting Filipino family could let its daughters go to school when they were surrounded by Japanese soldiers notorious for gang-raping nuns. Connie's family had lost everything, so their daughter could either find a menial job or work as a servant, in which case she would be expected to serve the sexual needs of the master, or his sons. Still in her teens, Connie thought Pete had been sent by heaven to change her life forever. He was unusually handsome and clean-cut, with clean habits, and had the kind of presence and look that made any normal girl weak in the knees. She had little experience with men, and Pete's aggressive love-making got her so excited she hardly remembered when she got all the bruises. She assumed she would spend the rest of her life with him, so she cooked and cleaned, and put up with his abuse as a small price.

Himself having grown up in extreme poverty, Pete regarded a backhand across the face as normal. He was like a rock, solid and confrontational. Phil, on the other hand, came from a family that punished only with words. More than once, trying to sleep on the couch, Phil had awakened to a quarrel in the bedroom that included loud whacks, yelps of pain, and cries of ecstasy, followed by whimpers. So he accepted Cheez's hotel room offer eagerly.

When Pete brought Connie to parties at the hotel, other guests thought she was a servant, or snubbed her. It was not working. One night, after another awkward party at the hotel, they returned to their apartment where Pete continued drinking. After midnight, he told Connie it was over. She wept, and pleaded. In desperation, she came out of the bathroom with scissors and stabbed Pete in the neck. An hour later, he arrived at the hotel suite drunk, bloody, and exhausted.

Now Pete was accepting Cheez's offer.

A few days later, word came from Connie's brother that she had swallowed poison, but survived. She was a mess. They heard nothing more for the moment, and thought Connie was now in the past.

Chapter 8 :

BREAKING THE RULES

"Things really began to happen after Cheez arrived," Phil exclaimed. "He was our new 'expediter' with a passion for living in grand style. The suite he rented had a separate bedroom for me. He insisted it was necessary as executives of JavaChina, since we were dealing with top U.S. Army brass. All at once our accommodations were luxurious, our dining lavish, and we had a bottomless expense account for entertaining guests -- both friends and business associates. Cheez also hired a gun-totting chauffeur to drive us around. And, thanks to Cheez, it was at the Manila Hotel that I met Nena Nieto."

Phil's first encounter with Nena was a social disaster, setting the stage for others to follow. More than just a gaffe, it drew attention to Phil as a zany troublemaker, and provoked the underworld bosses to go after him.

Never having stayed at Claridge's in London, the Ritz in Paris, the Vila Real in Madrid, or the Waldorf-Astoria in New York, Phil saw no reason to leave the barracks behind and adopt cotillion etiquette at the Manila Hotel. He had moved into the suite with Cheez just before Colonel Nieto took over as hotel manager, and was accustomed to the relaxed atmosphere around the swimming pool where you could still eat poolside, and in the Pavillion where you could have an informal lunch still in your bathingsuit.

But all that changed when Nieto clamped down. New rules of behavior were issued, poolside meals were prohibited, and bathingsuits were banned from the dining room. The colonel himself patrolled the perimeter in a suit and tie, with a silk scarf draped artfully over his shoulder, to make certain everyone behaved accordingly. Phil could not resist:

"One morning at the swimming pool, I was showing off, mocking the new manager, Colonel Nieto. I was mimicking his manner -- the way he would walk arrogantly around the hotel, an expensive silk scarf draped over his shoulder, grimacing at employees and glowering at clients like me. I had no idea that he was one of General MacArthur's cronies, not to mention one of the richest men in The Philippines." Or, more important in the long run, that he was a senior watcher for Lansdale at G-2, and for the Quirino Machine.

"Taking my eyes off The Colonel to see what kind of audience I had, I noticed a beautiful young woman watching my antics intently. With a look of burning anger she came stalking in my direction, drawing back her right fist. Knowing she was about to give me one hell of a wallop, I ducked my head and grabbed her raised arm. Then I tugged her off balance, pulled her to me, and gave her a little kiss. Like Rhett Butler and Scarlett." Had this happened at poolside in California, there might have been a ripple of applause. But in Manila Phil had just torn up the book of Spanish etiquette. The girl he had grabbed and kissed was the 23-year-old daughter of Colonel Nieto, the hotel manager. Her face turning scarlet, Nena left the pool in a rage. Not knowing who she was, Phil continued drawing stares. He looked good in his brief swimsuit. Even a bit rakish. Since leaving the ATC he had gained twenty pounds that he carried well, let his Army brush-cut grow out with the added touch of sideburns, and had grown a moustache.

"Around midday, some of us decided to order lunch poolside. A waiter told us this was not allowed by the management. We were sent to The Pavilion restaurant inside. I was with two girls who worked for the War Damage Commission and also lived at the Manila Hotel. We were all still in bathing suits. Colonel Nieto sent word that we would not be served until the girls covered up and the men put on dinner jackets.

"Waiting for a room clerk to bring me my jacket, I saw the same angry beautiful girl come into The Pavilion. To my surprise, she walked straight over and sat down at my table. By then the two other girls had reappeared in appropriate sundresses, and the room clerk brought me my jacket, which I put on -- still in my swimming trunks.

"It was silly and crude and doubtless I offended a lot of 'decent people' by what I was doing. You would never be served in a five-star restaurant in the United States dressed in swim trunks and a dinner jacket. But at the time I thought it was a good joke.

"Again, the waiter refused to take our order. I was about to get up and leave, when Nena countermanded the Colonel's order. She told the waiter to serve us lunch, which he promptly did."

At first Phil just stared at her, drinking her in. She was very beautiful, with high cheekbones and dark brown almond shaped eyes that sparked with life. About 5 feet 3 inches, around 130 pounds, she wore her dark hair swept up and pinned in place. Her hands were small and slender, nails and toenails perfectly manicured without garish lacquer. She needed no makeup, wore pearl earring studs but no other jewelry, and dressed in expensive simplicity. Despite the hot Manila weather, she looked cool and serene, having taken her anger in stride.

During that luncheon, Phil learned a bit about Nena. She was Colonel Nieto's daughter by his first marriage, and has been educated by nuns. Later, he would discover that she was not as self-assured as she appeared. She was used to being in the limelight because of her father, and cultivated attention from admirers, because she needed constant reassurance. She liked being stared at and expected others to cater to her. She gathered boyfriends and admirers, but kept them at arm's length. Solitude made her restless, so as a night owl she called in other young women to play mah-jong into the early morning hours. Gossip was her mainstay, which kept her in the loop on what was happening in Manila. She spoke Tagalog, English and Spanish but her soft voice turned raucous and guttural when she got mad.

When slighted, she was quick to take offense, as she had flared beside the pool.

Nena and Phil were never more than pals. When she was in the United States during the war, she had dated several movie stars in California and was courted by Nick Capone, brother of the Chicago mob boss. She led that spoiled and luxurious existence on the edge of a milieu of which Henry Miller said, "We were doing it like rabbits back then, too, we just didn't talk about it." Yet Nena seemed to be there in spirit but not in the flesh. She had been married briefly -- an experiment that failed. She separated immediately from her husband, of whom she never spoke. They were not divorced, because divorce was illegal in the Catholic Philippines, except for certain cases of adultery. Returning after the war to her family's privileged circumstances in The Philippines, with mansions in Manila, in Ilocos Norte, and in the mountain resort at Baguio, she grew bored and restless, but spent most of her time with girlfriends, and was not linked romantically with anyone at the time. She often threatened to fly off to Reno for a quickie divorce, but being divorced did not really matter if you were not leaping in and out of bed, and as a conspicuous member of one of the country's richest and highest ranking families she was stuck and knew it.

Phil's relationship with Nena was like a thorn in Colonel Nieto's paw. The Colonel regarded Phil as uncouth, undisciplined and rude. He was just a young American punk with money in his pocket. Even before Phil did his poolside impersonation, the Colonel had taken an instant dislike to him and everything he did. But Nena had leverage over her father. The Colonel knew his daughter knew he was cheating on his second wife (having arranged an annulment from his first). An uneasy truce existed between father and daughter.

Phil had now acquired another motorcycle, so in the coming weeks he sometimes took Nena out for rides around the countryside. That's all it was. She came home un-mussed. What seemed to attract her to Phil was his impetuous disregard for manners and propriety, and his utter certainty that whatever he did, it would work out for the best. There was no need for him to be careful. This fascinated Nena because it was precisely the opposite of everything she had been taught. From time to time his swashbuckling would wear thin on her, and she would lash out -- once hurling a leather bound book at him, gashing his eyebrow and leaving him with a small scar for the rest of his life. On the other hand, Nena would come to his rescue and effectively save his life.

Chapter 9 :

'IN IRONS'

The consequences of Phil's outrageous behavior at the Manila Hotel were not obvious, but word went out from Colonel Nieto to all branches of the Quirino Machine that Phil was to be watched, and punished. This added a dangerous and aggressive personal element to the surveillance already being conducted for Lansdale at G-2. It was one thing to be watching the two Americans and the Russian closely as probable communist agents, another thing entirely to have the pleasure of tripping them up, blocking their path, and driving them crazy. As word filtered down through the harbor police, the Seamen's Union, dockworkers, immigration and customs officers, and all levels of the underworld, you could hear lips smacking. After all, they were not Filipinos. They had no right to be here.

Before Cheez had arrived on the scene, Phil had started lining up captains and crews to take the JavaChina ships to Shanghai. Experienced American seafarers were going home, so good deep-water skippers and crews were hard to find. The Filipino merchant marine was still getting re-organized following the Japanese occupation, and most local sailors only had inter-island experience.

So, finding crews was taking time. Phil thought the hostility he now encountered was the result of anti-Americanism coming with independence. To him it was a new side to the Filipino mentality, pent-up anger released like steam from a pressure cooker. But he had little choice. They were now well into June. Further delays would take them deeper into the typhoon season, or 'wet hell'.

To hire crews legally, Phil had to go through the International Labor and Marine Union, everywhere an instant constituency for the underworld. In Manila this Seaman's Union was run by the Quirino Machine.

The union boss, a stocky toad known to his enemies as MadDog Mabini, already knew who Phil was, who he worked for in Shanghai, that he lived in the Manila Hotel, that he had been messing around with Colonel Nieto's daughter, and was being bankrolled by a Russian named

Cheez. Mabini went for maximum squeeze, and Phil did not have the time to haggle.

"We were far behind schedule. The Union demanded an advance cash payment to cover its 'expenses' and the crew's initial wages. This was just heavy-handed union tactics, but they knew we were desperate, so I had little choice but to comply."

Five Filipino skippers and crews were hired. Two of the captains were to prove honorable, while the other three selected by Mabini were planted as troublemakers who would blame everything on bad weather, bad luck, or JavaChina knowing nothing about ships and the sea.

Before a single F-boat was seaworthy, Winkelman added to Phil's grief by insisting on buying six surplus PT-boats, along with the two comparatively new F-boats, and a beautifully-built 68-foot 'air-rescue' craft that was like a motor yacht. The condition of the 80-foot PT-boats varied from poor to nearly-new. According to Pete, Winkelman originally wanted to buy the PT-boats for $2,000 each, insure them for $10,000, then sink them at sea and collect the profit. Whether or not this was true, Winkelman then decided to have the PT-boats towed to Shanghai for sale to Chinese buyers. With bureaucratic logic, Winkelman imagined that each 100-foot F-boat mini-freighter could tow two 80-foot PT-boats all the way to Shanghai even during typhoon season. Any seafarer could have told him that even in good weather, the F-boats would be strained towing more than one PT-boat. JavaChina's F-boats were in poor shape, and had only one large diesel engine, so if anything went wrong with the mother ship the babies in tow would be in peril. Winkelman's new plan meant that the first three F-boats ready to sail would first have to go south to the island of Samar -- where surplus PT-boats were kept -- each take two of them in tow, then make up the lost time by sailing directly north along the weatherly east coast of Luzon.

This exposed them to any typhoons that developed. Winkelman's thinking was based on profit, not common sense.

Despite their wartime glamor, PT-boats were not being sent back to the United States.

They were famous for daring high-speed attacks during the war, but they were cheaply made to be expendable, never intended for repair or salvage. Despite minor differences in design, all were about 80 feet in length, with a 21-foot beam and shallow draft. Their hulls were lightweight mahogany plywood, with a short life in tropical seas subject to dry rot or being eaten by teredo worms. Hundreds of the sleek torpedo-boats were retired to Base 17, near Bobon Point on Samar. In 1945, the most decrepit, already rotting and disintegrating, were stripped of motors and equipment, then beached and burned. The remaining ones were available practically free to anyone who would come get them. This was irresistible to Winkelman because these fast, shallow-draft boats were ideal for river trading and military operations in coastal China. No Dutch businessman could turn down a profit on near-zero investment. Nevertheless, as a precaution Winkelman had each PT-boat insured for $10,000 – tending to confirm Pete's suspicion that the JavaChina boss never really expected them to reach Shanghai.

The U.S. Navy had always warned that PT-boats were held together by "rivets, bolts, screws, and glue.... When one lets down, one of the others has to take added strain and eventually weakens. Under heavy going a minor weakness may develop into major damage. A taut ship is a happy ship, but there is no ship that will become un-taut quicker than a PT if you neglect her." To take one in tow, the Navy recommended using bridle-and-pendant gear to reduce the strain on its plywood bow.

If you had no bridle, a line could be attached to the sturdy Sampson Post in the bow, which was part of the boat's spine, but on a six-day sea voyage this was asking for trouble. Pete knew all about PT-boats, and was already in Samar choosing the best ones from the decaying flotilla at Boton Point. He had repaired them, and knew they had to be kept in thoroughbred racing form. But few of those at Bobon were still thoroughbreds. Luckily, Pete was able to acquire six virtually unused PT-boats.

Three of the five JavaChina F-boats were at last pronounced seaworthy by inspectors from Lloyds of London, and left Manila the first week of August, heading south to Samar. The U.S. Army's contractual deadline for repairs had been missed by two months. These three were the F-122, F-93, and F-77, each under the command of a Filipino captain and Filipino crew hand-picked by MadDog Mabini. The vessels did not travel in convoy, but left Manila at two-day intervals as last-minute repairs were completed. Even so, F-77 left without its crucial and mandatory radio gear.

Phil and Pete had worked their tails off to achieve the miracle, finding a lot of the equipment the hard way, doing much of the labor themselves. In the process, both young men had aged considerably, no longer looking 21 years old. It was no longer a labor of love. So they were in no mood to see things go wrong. The F-122, under Mabini's favorite, Captain Romero Dimuahuan, was the first to leave Manila and last to arrive in Shanghai. She should have been re-christened TARBABY.

Before the F-122 reached Shanghai, Captain Dimuahuan would go out of his way to do everything wrong, create legal problems, nearly get Phil murdered, land Phil and Cheez in prison, then bankrupt JavaChina, and saddle them with debts they could never pay. Four days after leaving Manila, Captain Dimuahuan sent a message saying F-122 had run low on oil -- despite extra stowed aboard in drums by Phil -- and was "obliged to deviate" from assigned course into the pretty harbor of Tacloban, in Leyte, the island next to Samar. F-93 had already sailed from Cavite along the same route south. Reacting instantly, Phil had just enough time to put extra oil aboard F-77, the third vessel, as she left Cavite. He ordered her captain to divert to Leyte to rendezvous with Dimuahuan and the F-122 there. Unfortunately, the F-77 had no radio, so these instructions could not be modified if things changed.

Phil flew directly to Samar to give Pete a hand rigging the PT-boats for tow. As if by magic, and without waiting for the extra oil to arrive, the F-122 then appeared in Samar with Dimuahuan acting like a hero.

The diversion of F-77 to Leyte with extra fuel was now only a waste of precious time, so Phil tried to get word to her skipper to bypass Leyte and make straight for Samar.

"Since she had no radio equipment, I came up with a plan to intercept her by small plane, dropping a message sealed in a coffee can. An Army pilot agreed to fly me out to the ship in a tiny AT-6 trainer.

"F-boats move slowly so we had a good idea where F-77 would be, and we did soon locate her. We circled her twice, then came in low over the ship at minimum speed. As we flew over the deck, I slid the cockpit canopy open and tossed out the coffee can, expecting it to fall onto the ship's deck. The plane's prop-wash caught the can and whipped it back in an arc to hit the plane's rudder. The can then spiraled down into the water and sank. In the process the can tore the fabric covering the plane's rudder. In a couple of minutes the fabric was shredding off in big strips. I was terrified as the rudder disintegrated. All I could think of was the little balsa wood gliders I had thrown as a child; when the rudder came off, they went into a tailspin and crashed. We scudded for Leyte and by the time we set down, the rudder fabric was gone. The pilot told me as long as he could use the ailerons on the wings to steer, he thought we would be okay. It would have been nice of him to mention this while we were in the air."

In Samar that evening, Phil and Pete inspected F-122, and were astonished and disgusted to see that Dimuahuan had turned her into "a God-damned floating whorehouse". Running low on oil had only been an excuse to party at Tacloban. Dimuahuan had taken the ship into various harbors along the way to Leyte to collect wives, sweethearts, and ladies-of-the-night, to keep himself and his crew happy on the voyage. His binge was financed by stopping in Tacloban to sell the ship's supplies, including her extra fuel oil. Making matters worse, his unscheduled stops and deviations from course broke the law, violating shipping rules designed to frustrate smugglers. Dimuahuan's antics would eventually cost JavaChina 5,000 pesos in fines, before the ship could be cleared again for Shanghai. Meanwhile, the F-122 would have to remain at anchor in Samar.

Even without radio equipment, the F-77 had now caught up and arrived in Leyte, apparently unaware that Phil and the Army pilot had buzzed the ship several times while trying fruitlessly to drop the message in the coffee can. Like Captain Dimuahuan, the skipper of the F-77 was an Ilocano. Checking on him in Leyte, they discovered that on reaching Tacloban he, too, had sold-off the extra oil Phil had put aboard in Manila to meet the 'emergency' on F-122. Phil and Pete were so mad they tracked down a Dutch captain to replace the F-77's Ilocano skipper and take the ship the rest of the way to Boton Point. The Dutchman had no credentials with Mabini's Seamen's Union, and cursed and abused the crew so much they went on strike, or what the British Admiralty would have called mutiny. In growing desperation, again without MadDog's okay, Pete asked a close Filipino friend, Captain Arroyo, to take command of F-77, a job he performed admirably, also to the satisfaction of the crew, while restoring the tarnished reputation of Filipino mariners in general. After weeks of delay caused by intrigues and sabotage, the three F-boats were at last rigged with tows.

Dimuahuan and his crew now claimed to be afraid to leave harbor, due to worsening weather.

Pete raged and ranted about how there was so far no typhoon alert, and the east coast of Luzon actually had plenty of sheltered harbors. He and Phil tried repeatedly to fire Dimuahuan, who said his job was protected by Mabini himself. That night Dimuahuan resorted to sabotage again by lighting up the entire ship for a party, burning out the main generator.

After midnight, he then ghosted F-122 out of Boton Point and slipped away once more to his home port of Tacloban in Leyte.

Had he not been protected by Mabini, Dimuahuan could have been arrested for repeated violations of Philippine maritime law, deviations from assigned course, vandalism and theft. Rather than arrest him, the authorities were supporting Mabini's mischief. The longer Dimuahuan could delay the voyage, the more MadDog could demand in wages, subsistence provisions, and advance payments of bribes. The contract Phil had been obliged to sign specified additional payments if the voyage was prolonged due to circumstances beyond the control of the captain or crew, such as equipment failure or bad weather. Dimuahuan could produce equipment failure on demand. For bad weather he only had to delay a few days. While the F-122 might be in irons, there was a chance of reaching Shanghai with the F-77 and F-93.

With PT-boats in tow, one-behind-the-other, they left Samar heading up the east coast of Luzon. Along the way, they had a hot date with Opal, who was not a lady.

Chapter 10 :

PORTS UNKNOWN

Typhoons usually hit The Philippines and China Sea between June and December, but in 1946 there was a series of freak typhoons out of season, including Typhoon Barbara in April, which had caught Phil and the PEONY offshore. Since then there had been Dolly, Elinor, Ginny, Ingrid, and others of varying intensity. Next in line was Typhoon Opal, which would wreak havoc on two of JavaChina's ships -- the F-77 and F-93 -- as they tried to tow PT-boats up the exposed east coast of Luzon.

The F-77 still had no radio, but its competent replacement Captain Jose Arroyo laid a course for China straight up the east coast of Luzon where he planned to cross the Taiwan Strait and make direct for the Yangtze estuary. In case Opal hit, he marked his charts with all the potential safe harbors along the way. It was the best he could do. He was not happy to be towing the PT-boats, but had no choice. His compatriot aboard the F-93 also was following those orders, so both skippers had tow-lines lashed to the Samson Posts at the bow of each PT-boat. It was a bizarre sight as the PT-boats were only 20 feet shorter than the mother ship, and were so lightweight that they danced in her wake, one PT-boat moving right while the next moved left, sometimes one surging forward in the restless sea, sometimes one dragging back. In a moderate sea it could be a losing battle. In a storm when Pacific rollers crest and break waves, the tow-lines might snap, or the PT-boats might ride up and smash to pieces on the mother ship's stern, or -- worse -- broach, fill with water, and sink -- causing the mother-ship to wallow and broach also.

Arroyo never had a chance to find out, for when Typhoon Opal struck the next night the two ships became separated, unable to maintain contact with only one radio between them. On the second night the tow-lines of both ships snapped like gunshots and all four PT-boats vanished like strangers in the night. Opal battered The Philippines for seven days, September 7-14, working her way up to Category-3 typhoon with sustained 100 mph winds. On the third day Arroyo's F-77 was driven ashore on remote Jomalig Island.

Throughout Typhoon Opal, Phil remained at the Manila Hotel awaiting a wire from Shanghai confirming the safe arrival there of the F-77 and F-93. On his 22nd birthday, September 19th, a bedraggled crewman staggered into Cheez's suite and handed Phil a sweat-stained, dog-eared letter written a week earlier:

Sir,

I have the honor to report that F-77 ran aground on the eastern coast of Jomalig Island, Lat. 14.26 Polilio, due to the strong typhoon in the locality on September 10th, 1946 at 7:25 P.M.

The two P.T. Boats we are towing were lost on the way during the strongest moment of the typhoon. I did my best to maneuver the ship, but the power of the ship was no match to the strength of the wind and waves which washed the ship to the shore. The Hull of the engine room was badly damaged and water penetrated, paralyzing the whole machineries therein.

No transportation connection to the island except small banca, and the nearest port is Polilio, which is 45 miles. Food supplies on board is enough for one week.

As regards the F-93, we were together on the way to shelter, but as the intensity of the typhoon reaches its peak and darkness approaches, we lost trace and have not heard since. Waiting for your orders the earliest possible time.

Very respectfully
Jose Arroyo
Capt. F-77

This letter had taken days to reach Phil. Arroyo's most trusted crewman had hired a native banca from fishermen on Jomalig Island, sailed it forty-five miles through rough seas to a big island called Polilio closer to the mainland, then hitched rides to the town of Daet where he caught a small plane to Manila. Flat broke by then, he hiked from the airport to the Manila Hotel.

It did not occur to him to get the news to Phil by phone. Captain Arroyo had told him to take the letter to Phil personally, as a matter of honor.

At this point, Phil felt certain the F-77 would remain forever on Jomalig Island. Some time in the future he would find his way to Jomalig to see if the damage could be repaired, otherwise remove everything of value, and let JavaChina pursue a claim at Lloyds for the insurance. Getting there would be difficult. Salvage would be impossibly expensive.

This bad news about F-77 made Phil gloomy, for he could only assume that F-93 also had been blown ashore somewhere, or sunk offshore by the typhoon, going down with all hands. He was in a black mood. Of the three ships he and Pete had made seaworthy, two were now lost, while the F-122 was kept in Leyte against his will. Nothing to celebrate.

The phone rang. Picking it up, he heard a distant crackling voice, the skipper of the F-93, who said he was calling from distant Quezon Province. His ship was okay. He said he had hugged the east coast of Luzon successfully, and not only survived, but made hundreds of miles to the north! Though battered by the typhoon and losing her two PT-boats, which might have saved her, the F-93 eventually reached the secure harbor of Baler, east of Cabanatuan City. There, he said, her overtaxed diesel engine had finally broken down. The captain said he was sorry about the engine needing repair, and the PT-boats vanishing.

When Cheez and Pete heard the news, all three were elated.

Baler was not Shanghai, but better than Davy Jones's Locker. Meanwhile, they could renew efforts to liberate the F-122 from Leyte. Pete agreed to go to Baler by plane immediately, to repair the diesel engine.

They were all angry with JavaChina, with Hertzka's foolishness, and Winkelman's folly. Getting stuck with the unscheduled PT-boat deliveries and then getting caught by Typhoon Opal. But in The Philippines there always was a coincidence of natural and unnatural disasters.

Chapter 11 :

WINKELMAN'S FOLLY

By the time Typhoon Opal had done its damage, it was the end of September 1946 -- three months past the promised U.S. Army delivery date for the original five vessels, plus the two newer F-boats bought as an afterthought. Pete had now flown off to Baler to fix the engine of the F-93.

Not one ship had yet reached Shanghai, so financial pressures were now biting Winkelman on the nose, as stiff contractual penalties forced him to pay angry Chinese buyers with money borrowed at a crippling 18 percent interest. Months would pass before Lloyds of London would pay the insurance claim on the F-77 blown ashore on Jomalig Island, its hull ripped open by rocks.

Captain Dimuahuan still strode the deck of the F-122 floating brothel in his home port of Tacloban, Leyte, under the protection of MadDog Mabini, while Phil sought vainly to get her out of legal irons. Four of the six PT-boats had broken loose and either sank or drifted off into the unknown. In Cavite, the U.S. Army was still refitting JavaChina's remaining ships, before they could be inspected for seaworthiness by Lloyds.

The financial squeeze on JavaChina tightened further as the economy of Nationalist China continued its collapse. One U.S. dollar was now officially worth 21,000 Nationalist dollars, or 43,000 on the black-market. In another half-hearted attempt to stop the hemorrhage of sound foreign currency fleeing China, the Nationalist regime made it illegal to export any U.S. dollars. Dr. Samet had to find new ways to smuggle U.S. currency to Manila, if Phil, Pete and Cheez were to receive their salaries plus extra funds to pay the mounting fines. Suddenly, Phil had an epiphany:

"Rather than wait longer for the U.S. Army to finish its work, which was hopeless, we would only have them get the ships' mechanical parts running, put all the remaining equipment in their holds, and I would deliver the last four ships to Shanghai, leading a single flotilla. Whatever re-outfitting remained to be done could be accomplished faster and better in Shanghai. If we did this immediately, we might get to Shanghai before October 1st, when more penalties would kick in."

The last freighters were only missing equipment that was sitting on the dock waiting to be installed. It could be hoisted aboard and stowed away. To be rid of the nuisance, the Army agreed to make them seaworthy enough to pass inspection. Getting them to Shanghai was Phil's problem.

"A sympathetic Army Captain gave us space at an Army dock in Manila, where we loaded the ships as fast as they passed inspection.

"A Chinese restaurant owner provided food for our crews for a week. We still had trouble finding competent captains, but we hired three Filipinos and an Australian named George Cowan. Rounding out the roster, I took command of the convoy aboard the lead ship."

These ships were numbered F-96, F-79, F-55, and F-92. While they were being cleared to sail, Phil fought a rear-guard action. The mischievous Captain Dimuahuan, encouraged by MadDog Mabini, now had filed a formal complaint against JavaChina for "unpaid wages owed" to himself and his hard-shagging crew during their long vacation island-hopping and women-hopping aboard the F-122. There were also rumblings from the truculent ex-captain of the F-77, relieved of command so quickly by Phil that it took Mabini off-guard. With Mabini's encouragement, the sacked skipper was trying to come up with charges to add to those of the rascal Dimuahuan.

With all these allegations hanging over his head, Phil could not risk asking police, tax, and immigration authorities for an exit visa to accompany the convoy to Shanghai. He knew Mabini was having him watched. Although he was only an employee of JavaChina, the Philippine authorities declared him to be a principal of the company, and would refuse him an exit visa. He had no choice but to go without a visa.

Saturday morning, September 28, 1946, four days after Phil's inception of the plan, the U.S. Army and Lloyds miraculously completed their final inspections and released the last of the four freighters.

The Customs office closed at noon on Saturdays, which left no time to clear all four the usual way. However, having lost his innocence over recent months, along with most other illusions, bribery was no longer an obstacle. In Manila, anyone seeking 'compliance' with Customs regulations just slipped cash between the pages of a ledger in the Customs office, making sure the bills stuck out far enough for even a zombie to recognize a bribe. You then left the room to allow your Tea Money to brew and vanish. On your return, the Customs staff cheerfully had your papers ready, their haste and ingenuity commensurate with the size of the bribe. Fifty pesos usually did the trick, like passing the police a $21-bill with your driver's license.

"Dropping all pretense, I approached the chief Customs officer and pledged several hundred pesos to him, plus double-overtime for his entire staff, if they would remain long enough to clear all four ships. He agreed. Since I had no exit visa, I slipped him an extra hundred pesos to allow me to depart without one."

Mabini had men watching outside, but Phil assumed his deal with the Customs chief was done inside, so it was strictly private. What he did not know was that G-2 also had him under close surveillance. Before the ships left Manila that evening, radiograms were flying.

Leading the convoy was Captain Vilamor on F-96, an Ilocano hired through Mabini. Vilamor was a seasoned officer in his mid-forties, a solidly built man about 5 feet 6 inches, but very headstrong.

Second in the column was F-79 under Captain Gisbert, a reliable man without Ilocano ties, but who would follow orders from whoever shouted loudest.

Third came Captain Cowan, a formidable Australian professional aboard the F-55, who had a low opinion of Filipino mariners.

Phil brought up the rear on the F-92 with Captain Hernandez at the helm, which enabled Phil to remain 'officially' out of sight.

After clearing Corregidor Island and the tip of the Bataan Peninsula, they turned north along Luzon's west coast. Not towing PT-boats, they made decent headway. However, no ship in the convoy had a radio.

"Since we were without radios, I told the captains to spread the column far enough to avoid any risk of collision, but to stay within sight of each other. Our only communication would be semaphore by flags or Morse Code by handheld signal lights.

Though I had just met Cowan, instinctively I had confidence in him. Cowan also had a very capable Chief Engineer with him, which alone can make or break a voyage. Privately, I had told Cowan that if anything happened to me, he was to take over as Fleet Commander. I gave him a letter to back this up. But later, as it turned out, that didn't stop Vilamor from trying to pull seniority, having been hired first. "

At dawn September 30, while rounding Cape Bolinao, Vilamor's lead ship slowed, and the column closed up. Vilamor said he had engine problems.

"Not wanting the convoy to separate, I signaled the rest of the ships to stand by to help the 96.

"With strong winds and ocean currents, the four ships began to drift westward into the South China Sea. When Vilamor signaled he was ready again to proceed, our motor on the F-92 refused to restart. My Chief Engineer assured me the trouble was minor and would only take a few minutes to fix. I had chosen this ship for myself because it was the fastest. I didn't want us all drifting farther off course, so I signaled Cowan to take the lead and proceed with the other ships. We would catch up."

Phil and his crew remained adrift on the 92, the ship heaving and sighing in the swells, while the 96, 79 and 55 continued up the coast of Luzon on their way toward Shanghai.

After working 24 hours in the intense heat of the engine room, with no rest and lots of profanity, Phil's Chief Engineer and his two grease-monkeys got the snarling diesel started. By then, the 92 had drifted sixty miles south and west. Phil set a new course due east to benefit from ocean currents nearer to Luzon. Before dawn the next morning, as they turned north to catch up with the convoy, a gale broke and visibility dropped nearly to zero. The gale lasted all day and night.

Phil had not been able to take a sextant sighting for two days. Next day, as the morning sun burned off the haze, he recognized two large islands off to starboard. He realized they had already cleared the northern tip of Luzon without knowing it, and were now 270 miles north of Cape Bolinao, making good headway toward Taiwan at full speed, on a bearing that would take them across the Formosa Strait. Phil's instincts as a navigator had returned with a great sense of exhilaration, after months of struggling with red tape, idiots, and troublemakers. He assumed that Captain Cowan and the others were now well ahead of him.

With clearing weather, and afforded some protection from easterlies by the island of Taiwan, they made rapid progress northwestward up the Taiwan Strait and entered the jade green East China Sea on the morning of October 4, making a steady eight knots. As midday approached under a hot sun, Phil went below for lunch and to write a letter home. After an hour, he sensed that something had changed. The ship, which had been riding steady all day, was now beginning to wallow. He went topside immediately. The sky had turned from clear blue to a dull saffron. The deep green swells were gone, replaced by oily troughs with gray beards and white teeth.

In the wheelhouse, Captain Hernandez was staring grimly at the barometer.

"The glass is falling steadily," he said.

A strong breeze was now gusting out of the northeast.

"Guess we're in for a storm," Phil replied.

Hernandez nodded toward the starboard bow where the sky was turning black. "This I don't like," he said. Phil did a quick inspection of 92 to make sure everything was secure. By the time he returned to the bridge, the small freighter was being tossed around by a rising sea.

Crew on deck began to lurch as if drunk, while staring at the black sky and crossing themselves. Most of these Filipinos had never sailed this far from land.

"I thought our small crew might feel more secure on the bridge, and gave the order. Soon most of them were crowded into the wheel house, except those on duty in the engine room. If we lost engine power, we would have to use a sea anchor to stabilize the ship."

The wind let up briefly as the eye of the storm passed over them. Then the full ferocity hit. All sense of time and direction were lost. Exhausted from puking, men were strewn across the floor of the bridge like broken matches. The storm howled and battered for three days and nights.

"All I could think of -- not for the first time -- was nobody would believe that waves can get so big." When the storm ended, just before dawn of the fourth day, the crew began stumbling out of the bridge, praying aloud in Tagalog. They were shocked to see that all the lifeboats were gone, including all deck cargo that had not been lashed down. As dawn came, they were treated to a breathtaking sight, as everything changed from slate black to vivid color. That afternoon, the blue-green coastline of China appeared to port.

"Against my better judgment, I decided to accommodate the crew and seek a safe anchorage while we cleaned up the ship. It was a mistake. I pored over the charts as we maneuvered through small islands with sheer rock cliffs. With only forty-five minutes of daylight left, we were in a deadly maze of reefs and islets where there was no sanctuary, no anchorage. So I changed my mind and ordered Hernandez to make for open sea."

Hernandez set a suitable course, but night came before they reached open water. At any moment they could hit a reef -- but that was not their only fear. Other dangers lurked among the islands.

These waters north of Amoy (Xiamen) on the mainland were a notorious traditional haven for Hokkien Chinese raiders. It would be a misnomer to call them either pirates or fishermen, because they changed from one to the other depending on what kind of prey was available for harvesting. When they were not pirates, they fished. When easy prey appeared on the surface, they stopped fishing.

Phil posted a watch bow and stern. During the night a small agile vessel started following them, a black shape they guessed was a diesel-powered junk of the type called Scrambling Dragons. With the 92's top speed of only eight knots, she was being overtaken gradually. Absent a radio, they had no way to get help. Before dawn, Phil had the Chinese flag of the 92's new owner lowered, and hoisted the ship's former U.S. Army Transport Corps flag. He wrapped black canvas around a broom, and erected it on the bow where from a distance it was a fair approximation of the .50 caliber machinegun typically mounted on U.S. Army ships. At daybreak, Phil turned the 92 broadside to their pursuer to hide the Chinese name on her stern. On his orders, the crew brought topside every firearm on board: one Enfield rifle, Phil's ivory-handled Colt .45 automatic, his tiny hideaway .32 Webley automatic, and an odd-looking pistol Captain Hernandez owned.

Individually, these were only pop-guns, but he had a plan. To emulate .50 calibre machine-gun fire, Phil counted to three, and all their weapons were fired simultaneously at the marauder's bow. The Scrambling Dragon immediately bore off. Slowing, it then followed for a while at a safe distance, then as a hazy sun rose veered off toward shore. Whoever the predators were, they had lost their nerve.

That afternoon, the 92 entered the Yangtze River delta with no further trouble. Having left The Philippines without a proper exit permit, Phil preferred not to stop for Customs. In the haze, they managed to glide past the Customs buoy unnoticed and into the Yangtze. His crew was exhausted, and desperate for a good meal. By the time they covered the forty-two miles to the confluence of the Yangtze and Whangpoo rivers the sun had set again. Sixteen miles remained to Shanghai. Phil decided not to risk it in the dark without a Chinese pilot, but to anchor here for the night. Early the following morning, October 9, still not hiring a pilot, they made the final leg to the Shanghai docks on their own, moving swiftly on an incoming tide. Their approach around a bend to the Shanghai Bund was, as ever, a spectacular sight. When JavaChina's office building came into view, Phil rashly gave a series of blasts on the ship's horn. Moments later, he saw chubby Dr. Samet running toward them with arms flapping and his fat belly bouncing up and down.

Phil telegraphed the engine room "full-speed-reverse" but the ship was carried on by the strong tide.

"I began to regret blasting the ship's horn. I wanted as little attention as possible while turning the ship around. In desperation, I ordered the crew to drop anchor, hoping to let the current turn us around. Our wake set scores of sampans bobbing and banging into one another. Dr. Samet was still flapping his arms and shouting, 'You made it... my God, you made it!' "

Samet was jubilant because JavaChina had no news whatever from the other three ships that had left Manila in convoy with Phil. Samet had sent many frantic messages to Manila, but the vessels had no radios, so no one knew what had become of them. The worst-case scenario was that the other three ships had gone down in the big storm. But right now what nearly made Samet burst a blood vessel was the first successful delivery, the first victory.

Seven months had passed since Felix Hertzka had signed the ill-fated contract for the five derelict F-boats. Three very costly, painful, frustrating months had passed since the original June delivery deadline had passed. For the moment, all this could be put aside in exhilaration.

"Samet was so excited he was almost blathering. We were presumed lost at sea; a search and rescue operation had been mounted; Philippine Air Line and U.S. Army planes criss-crossed the China Sea looking for us." He rushed back to his office to notify their Chinese purchasers. Less than thirty minutes after tying up, 92 was invaded by Chinese men in suits and ties, with pads, pencils, rulers, calipers and measuring tapes.

They dashed from place to place chattering excitedly in Shanghai dialect, pausing only to scribble tiny Chinese characters on their pads, like ancient hieroglyphs, then dash to another spot. Taking nothing for granted, they constantly rolled and unrolled blueprints of the vessel provided by Dr. Samet.

"Samet introduced me to the Chinese clients. In spite of our missing the delivery deadline, they were so desperate for small freighters that all was forgiven." Everyone was overwhelmingly friendly.

Phil had been days without sleep. All he wanted was a soft mattress. But the clients, as all Chinese seem able to do at a moment's notice, had arranged a banquet.

Cleaning up quickly and changing clothes, he went to the banquet and was, he said, "received like a prince". When green tea was served he appalled his hosts by asking for cream. Dinner was strange and non-stop. Downing a huge meal because he was starving, Phil pleased his hosts. Then, dog-tired, he excused himself to head for bed. Before he could sleep, Samet dashed in, puffing with more news.

The good news was that the other three ships -- 96, 79 and 55 -- were all in a safe harbor. The bad news was that the harbor was Salamague, way back on the west coast of Luzon. Phil would have to return to Manila immediately to get those ships underway to Shanghai. Though grateful for the successful first delivery, the Chinese clients had made it clear to Samet after the feast that they expected Phil, the magician, to deliver those other ships straight away. This was harder to swallow than anything at the banquet.

"I headed back to my room hoping to get in at least a few hours of rest. I felt slightly ill but figured it was just fatigue. I had barely closed my eyes when I realized it was more than that. After living for days on salted fish, the huge banquet -- and the unfamiliar things in it -- made me deathly ill and I spent the night in misery. Next morning, I dragged myself out of bed to obtain an exit visa from China, plus an entrance visa to The Philippines, and caught the first available flight."

Cheez met his plane in Manila. The good news was that a second F-boat. the F-93 brought by Pete from Baler, had reached Shanghai. The bad news was that Pete had then quit.

Chapter 12 :

PETE GETS SPOOKED

Just before Phil had left Manila with the JavaChina convoy, Pete had flown to Baler on the east coast of Luzon to finish engine repairs on the stranded F-93. This would take several days, which he wanted to spend quietly in a silent engine room, without the Filipino captain and crew around to annoy him. Hitching up his holstered side-arms -- he had replaced his Army 45s with two Smith & Wesson .357 magnums -- Pete told the captain to go have a party, get lost. Then he gave the crew liberty on the understanding that they would remain in the harbor in case he needed them. Then he took his canvas bag of precious tools and went below, where it was cool because the engine had not run in weeks. There was a lot he wanted to think about. During the months they had shared lodging and worked together as partners and comrades on ATC ships and JavaChina deliveries, Pete and Phil had watched each other's backs like gunslingers in the Wild Wild East. In places like Manila, where everybody was desperate, you needed a sidekick. Peterson had been at the wrong end of a lethal weapon often enough to know when he was a target. Two recent events had made him very uneasy.

Only now did he have time to mull it over.

He recalled the afternoon when Phil had returned to their suite at the Manila Hotel, Cheez had greeted him in George Raft gangster movie style:

"You got trouble boy! Three lawmen are looking for you. They're down in the lobby waiting. Didn't say what they wanted."

Phil called the front desk and had the trio sent up -- an American and two Filipinos from the Counter-Intelligence Corps of G-2. The American spoke in a thick Brooklyn accent:

"Name's Freight. Mind if we come in and ask some questions?" Freight sat, and came to the point.

"Last three or four days we been investigatin' you and your partner Peterson. We want to talk to you about some stolen property."

"What stolen property?"

"Stuff you cached away in a garage: engine parts, motorcycles, a lot of other stuff."

"You fellows got a warrant?"

"No, but we could, easy.

"We wanted to finish investigatin' first, then talk to you."

"So you're not sure the stuff was stolen, right?"

"Look, you gotta admit you and your whole setup looks mighty phony."

Cheez, more alert and prepared than he looked, waved a sheaf of papers at Phil: receipts for all the surplus Jeeps, motorcycles, and other equipment they had purchased. Phil handed them to Freight.

"Maybe you ought to look these over first."

Freight thumbed through the receipts.

Phil snickered: "Whoever told you this stuff was stolen gave you a bum steer. So, who's pointing the finger anyway?"

"That Filipino gal, Connie Something, friend of your pal Peterson. She took us to the garage, and the other address where we spotted the Jeeps."

One of the Filipino detectives was still holding the papers. Cheez snatched them from him, and snorted at Freight.

"Just as I thought. She acted in spite, because Peterson dumped her."

"Okay, so she put the finger on you. Not our fault."

When he heard about this later, Pete shrugged and muttered a few curses about 'women'. But he really could not believe Cheez's easy explanation that this was only the result of Connie's being a woman-scorned. There had to be more to it.

"What bothers me is that G-2 took so much interest in a little Army surplus. They were probably fishing for us. Why?"

Not long after Freight's visit, Pete's antennas tingled again when he went with Phil to see MadDog Mabini. Unlike Freight, Mabini had them in a hammerlock, and seemed to be protected from any counterattack. Pete had wondered who was behind Mabini's bluster. Phil for his part remembers being "really afraid" of Mabini and his thugs.

Back when Pete and Phil learned they could only hire Filipino captains and crews through Mabini, they thought he was a small-fry local union boss.

Even so, to 'expedite' hiring, they had handed Mabini 11,000 pesos (over $5,000) in return for a receipt scribbled on a torn envelope.

MadDog insisted all contracts required deducting union dues and commissions before wages were paid to the men. Running a union was hard, he said, because Filipinos were so unreliable. In the end none of the money was passed on to the crews they hired.

Neither Phil nor Pete realized that Mabini ran the union for the Quirino Machine, as an extortion racket to squeeze shipowners and crews. Given how poor most seamen were, with wives and children to support, this racket was scraping the bottom of the barrel. The way things worked throughout Asia was 'tax farming' -- getting control of as many rackets as you could, then 'farming' them for payoffs and protection. Rajahs, warlords, prime ministers and presidents gave their supporters -- like Mabini -- certain tax farming privileges in return for their loyalty.

Only a few days after they gave the 11,000 pesos to Mabini, one of the Filipino captains they had hired came to Phil, hat in hand, to ask when he and his men would be paid. Phil was stunned. "I gave your union boss, Mabini, 11,000 pesos more than a week ago to pay you and the crews."

The man shook his head.

"You say so, but we got no money."

Phil went straight to Mabini, who was evasive.

"Don't worry, Captain Mehan, the crews get what's coming to them." A well-rehearsed line.

Phil told him the crews would quit if they did not get their money now. Mabini knew better, and smiled.

"Look, Captain Mehan, I take care of union business. You hire crews from me and the crews have a contract with the union. Once I have the paperwork done, and have deducted the dues and commissions, everything will be okay. It's union business."

The crews and skippers cared nothing of union business, but they did want their money. Phil went back to Mabini.

"Captain Mehan, these men are not educated. They do not understand how their contract with my union works. I find them jobs and there are certain expenses and deductions; insurance, license fees and such things. This I take from the wages when the work starts." So long as the ships were not ready to sail, he said, captains and crews were not yet working.

But they had wives, hungry families, and debts.

"I'm going to the police and have you arrested for swindling."

Mabini sneered. "Don't be hasty."

The union boss soon found a way to strike back.

Mabini began sending drunken seamen to the Manila Hotel. In the lobby, Phil was harassed by the drunks demanding wages. Each time he left the hotel, he was surrounded by crew who were little more than besotted beggars.

On two separate occasions, late at night, sailors invaded the hotel. The doormen whose main job was to keep out riffraff were in on it, and gave the men Phil's original room number.

Storming up to the room, they pounded on the door, uttering threats and screaming for their money. That room was now occupied by a U.S. Senator, whose romance was disturbed. The second time a U.S. Congressman was disturbed. After the second incident, Colonel Nieto ordered Phil to vacate the hotel. Nena countermanded the order, reminding her father that if provoked Phil might blab about the Colonel's extramarital flings. You could see fumes coming out the Colonel's ears.

Meanwhile, Phil went to the District Attorney and got a warrant for Mabini's arrest for embezzlement. Tipped off by the District Attorney's office, MadDog disappeared for a few weeks, till Phil and Pete were busy elsewhere. Everybody was tipped off in advance.

Phil had demanded a meeting with the president of the Seamen's Union, Jacinto Salazar, imagining that Salazar was not just a figurehead. Phil told Salazar that the union had failed in its obligation to provide disciplined crews and trustworthy skippers, so he should reimburse JavaChina for non-performance, also he must reimburse fines Phil had paid for their course deviations, and unauthorized port calls of Captain Dimuahuan and Captain Vilamor.

Phil also had to pay a 5,000 peso fine to clear F-122 again for departure to China.

Brushing this aside, Salazar cited 'international law'. If Phil was unhappy with the way the union did its job, JavaChina would have to pay the contract regardless. There would be no refund.

Salazar insisted that Phil meet union members face-to-face, including some of the crewmen assigned by Mabini, to negotiate a resolution of

JavaChina's 'debt'. To put him at a further disadvantage, Phil would have to negotiate in Tagalog. He knew only enough Tagalog for taxis and restaurants. So Phil brought his pal Gus Vellejo, director of the Manila office of Philippine Air Lines.

Arriving for the meeting, they were confronted by a hostile crowd, coached in advance by Mabini. Gus pulled Phil outside for a talk. Being Filipino, he was all too familiar with shakedowns. Being educated, handsome and gay, at a time when gay was not tolerated, Gus was trembling, his face ashen. He told Phil he had heard union thugs say they would murder Phil if he did not pay up. Phil shrugged. He explained that JavaChina had turned off the tap, because of the freeze on hard currency leaving China, so he was now broke. No one in the union hall would ever get another penny.

"Tell 'em, if they kill me, they won't get anything." Gus went back inside and conveyed the message in Tagalog, to delay Phil's murder.

Returning to the union office to retrieve some papers, Phil saw a sweaty MadDog dangling two 100 peso notes under the nose of a female clerk, offering her money for some immediate sexual favors. Phil snatched the money out of MadDog's fingers.

"You owe me 11,000 pesos. These are on account." Startled, Mabini turned, eyes like a cobra.

Phil jabbed a finger in Mabini's face and announced to the entire office:

"There's a warrant for your arrest at the police station."

He saw a policeman sitting at the back of the room.

"Officer, arrest this criminal!"

"Ah, but Captain Phil, that's Mabini!"

A few days later Pete, still hot about Mabini's swindle, saw MadDog and two other men coming his way along the Manila Bay seawall. Pete pulled both his magnums from his gunbelt, released the safeties, and aimed at Mabini.

"We're going to police headquarters to straighten out this mess."

Mabini's companions, who had drifted off slightly, now pulled out burp guns. Small and easy to conceal under a loose Barong, burp guns were fully automatic and fired .45 calibre rounds from a long clip that at close range could rip a man to shreds in seconds. But this was a

Mexican Standoff. Phil appeared from the street a moment later and hustled Pete away before any shots were exchanged.

Brooding in the quiet of the engine room over these bad scenes, and many others, Pete began to see a bigger, more sinister picture emerging of what was going on behind the curtains. Having seen action in the war, with more than one vessel blown out from under him by the Japanese, Pete's instincts and intuitions were finely honed to danger. He realized that the Big Fish had them under surveillance, manipulating them through men like Mabini, sabotaging their efforts through bastards like Dimuahuan.

This could even involve the connivance of greedy U.S. Army officers at Cavite who were deliberately delaying repairs. Maybe even had the encouragement of General MacArthur's clique. Pete knew G-2 was watching them and meddling, because they had been questioned at the hotel by the agent named Freight.

However, Pete would never have guessed the true magnitude of G-2's surveillance. He knew G-2 could be misguided, boneheaded, and stupid, but the idea of his pals being a communist cell was too bizarre and farfetched ever to cross his mind. Nevertheless, he knew bad things were coming, from the itching in his thumbs. Some time soon, Pete decided, he and Phil were going to be ambushed and salted away like codfish. What would happen then he could only guess. But it would be bad, worse because they would forfeit their liberty and any chance to strike back. Pete was a man who valued his liberty above all. He had learned long ago to trust his intuition. Now he decided it was time to get out of The Philippines forever. Maybe out of China, too, before it fell to a new government. As if to agree, the diesel engine responded to its glow-plugs and started instantly.

Pete was rarely frightened, but now he was really spooked.

Rather than returning the F-93 to the command of her Filipino captain, still partying somewhere in Baler, Pete took command himself as owner's representative, called the crew aboard from bars and brothels around the harbor, and weighed anchor immediately for Shanghai.

Screw the Philippine maritime authorities, who had helped bugger-up everything, intentionally or by sheer incompetence. Somewhere in the China Sea, he unknowingly crossed wakes with Phil's F-92, reaching Shanghai just after Phil boarded the plane for Manila.

Pete breathed a sigh of relief to be back in China. Odd as it might seem, he knew his chances were better in the chaos of a Chinese civil war, than in the peaceful democracy of the Americanized Philippines.

The first thing he did in Shanghai was to storm into the offices of JavaChina, magnums drawn. Only the fact that Winkelman was still in San Francisco kept Pete from shooting him in the knees. Instead he confronted Dr. Samet and gave him the ass-chewing he had planned to give Winkelman.

It was all too clear to Pete now that Winkelman was responsible for a lot of their grief. The Dutchman could blame Hertzka for naively signing a blank contract, which allowed the U.S. Army to choose ships in horrible condition, then drag its feet outfitting them, so Phil and Pete missed all their delivery deadlines. But Winkelman should not have let Hertzka be given such a crucial mission. Then Winkelman made it all infinitely worse by purchasing the two extra F-boats, the Crash-Boat, the PT-boats, insisting that the PT-boats be towed to Shanghai in the midst of typhoon season. Winkelman was hanging an albatross around their necks, putting Pete and Phil in serious danger. It galled Pete especially that Winkelman then blamed them as 'adolescents' for putting JavaChina in serious financial jeopardy.

It was also Winkelman who had chosen Cheez to 'expedite' the transfers, and entrusted Cheez with nearly a quarter of a million dollars in cash. He should have known Cheez was a lousy businessman and half-hearted accountant. Only a fool would put a gregarious Russian in charge of money.

Faced with all these charges, Dr. Samet crumpled, acknowledged Pete was right, and turned over the back-wages and expenses owed to him.

Kissing JavaChina goodbye, without regrets, Pete rented an apartment in Shanghai's International Settlement and wrote to Phil that he was accepting a great job-offer from the United Nations Relief Organization, to instruct Chinese in fishing with trawlers. Not long afterward, Phil heard that Pete had fallen in love and married a pretty Czech refugee he'd just met -- a marriage that would last more than half a century. Phil could hardly believe his pal and sidekick had kept this romance and engagement secret. He wrote home, only half in jest:

"I don't think I have recovered from the shock. I might have known something like this would happen should I leave him alone."

He missed Pete's wild and hot-headed company. Likable as Cheez was, you could not expect him to fill Pete's boots.

Chapter 13 :

TAKING CHARGE

Pete's decision to flee The Philippines happened so fast there was no time to explain it, and nobody around to listen. Phil was in Shanghai at the time, too distracted by ship-delivery problems to figure out why things kept going wrong. Next on Phil's plate was to find out what had happened to the three other ships in his convoy, and get them to Shanghai. With Pete gone, and Cheez managing things in Manila, Phil would have to sort things out himself. He had no idea why Captain Cowan and the two Filipino captains -- Vilamor and Gisbert -- had not sought shelter in Taiwan but had gone back to Luzon, to a bay near Vigan, the birthplace of the Quirino brothers.

In fact, Captain Cowan, the Australian, was mad as hell about this back-tracking. He had signaled repeatedly for the other ships to continue north to Taiwan with him, but was ignored by Captain Vilamor, who seemed to dominate Captain Gisbert. So, to keep the convoy together, Cowan grudgingly accompanied the other two back to Luzon. Once anchored side by side in the bay near Vigan, Cowan had a shouting match with Vilamor across the space between their ships.

Vilamor claimed seniority by asserting falsely that he had more sea-time, and had been placed by Captain Mehan at the head of the convoy column, making him the convoy commander:

"If anyone should take command of the fleet in the absence of Captain Mehan," Vilamor shouted, "it should be me."

Cowan tried to get Vilamor to read the letter Phil had left designating the Australian as his replacement, but Vilamor rudely turned his back.

Vilamor then went ashore and caught a ride to Vigan, accompanied by his first mate, ostensibly to borrow 300 pesos from a nephew to restock provisions before continuing to Shanghai. Actually, he went to report to the Quirinos.

Whether Cowan suspected foul play, or was just fed up, he put his own first mate in charge of Vilamor's F-96, got the mild Captain Gisbert's full attention with an explosion of Australian curses, and moved the three ships a few miles north to a smaller bay at Salomague, so Vilamor and his first mate would return to find the ships gone. Cowan figured they could "get stuffed".

Once the weather calmed, Cowan prepared to depart Salomague for Shanghai on his F-55. He would leave Vilamor's F-96 in Salomague to be sorted out later. But he encouraged Gisbert on the F-79 to go with him to Shanghai. The meek Captain Gisbert agreed at first then, after following Cowan up the coast a few miles, lost his nerve, flashed a signal that he had a burned-out engine bearing, and was going back to the U.S. Navy base at Subic Bay for repairs.

Naturally, as a Filipino, Gisbert had misgivings about defying Captain Vilamor and the Quirinos. Although it was obvious he could not get to Subic with a burned-out bearing, Cowan shrugged and wrote him off, continuing on his way to China with the F-55.

Knowing none of this, Phil thought all three ships were still at Vigan. So, on his arrival at Manila Airport he caught the next domestic flight to the Ilocos. He felt he had broken the JavaChina jinx by delivering one ship, so he was in a mood to kick some ass.

Phil was going right into the Ilocano stronghold, where disputes were sometimes settled with flame-throwers at twenty paces. He knew they were being sabotaged, but as yet he had no idea who was behind it, or that he was personally targeted by the Quirino Machine. He still imagined that his biggest enemy was MadDog Mabini. He never guessed that G-2 agents were watching his every move, and that his real enemy was the ambitious Lansdale.

Landing in the provincial town of Vigan, Phil easily located Captain Vilamor and summarily fired him for disobeying owners' instructions. Then he hired a Jitney – half Jeep, half Model-T – and loaded it with provisions. Anxious to get out of Vigan before sundown, he did not haggle over prices. You could eat well-enough in The Philippines for a dollar a day, so he spent $500 on enough groceries for a week's voyage. When the Jitney was packed, Phil told the driver to take him to Salomague, where he discovered only one ship: Vilamor's F-96. The other two freighters had left earlier, apparently both for Shanghai.

Explaining nothing, he ordered the supplies put aboard. The crew complied, each sailor carrying a sack of food on his head out the short jetty to the ship. Then Phil commanded them to hoist anchor. Motoring out into a calm China Sea, he set a course directly across the Taiwan Strait from Salamague to the Yangtze, no stops along the way.

After seven days of decent weather, the F-96 reached Shanghai only an hour after Captain Cowan's F-55, which had taken a less direct route. JavaChina was jubilant.

His dander up now, Phil resolved to bring the last two freighters to Shanghai: Gisbert's F-79 at Subic Bay, and Dimuahuan's F-122 at Tacloban. No more nonsense. Phil and Cowan caught the same plane back to Manila. During the flight, Phil instructed Cowan to accompany him onward to Tacloban to rescue the F-122 from Captain Dimuahuan.

While the ship had been confined to port at Tacloban, Phil had managed to get repairs made to her, so she was ready to go. Cowan would take her from Tacloban to Manila. Meantime, Phil would fly to Subic Bay, get matters sorted out with Captain Gisbert, so Cowan and Gisbert could rendezvous and take the last two vessels -- F-122 and F-55 -- to China before there was anymore trouble. They had to move as fast as possible to take everyone off-guard. Like a good omen, when they disembarked at Manila Airport, there was a domestic flight just boarding for Tacloban. It was beginning to feel like he was on a roll.

Being tough felt good.

As planned, the F-122 and F-55 reached Shanghai without difficulty early in December 1946, six months overdue. In Manila, Phil and Cheez celebrated the successful delivery of all JavaChina vessels except the storm-wrecked F-77, which was covered by Lloyds insurance.

As relief sank in, Phil had time to take stock.

Only one significant problem remained: to conclude the insurance claim with Lloyds of London for the wrecked F-77. JavaChina was now desperate for money, and the only thing holding up their insurance check was Lloyd's insistence on seeing photographs of actual damage to the F-77. Phil would have to go personally to remote Jomalig Island with a camera. And at the same time, he and Cheez might also be able to raise some personal cash by salvaging the cargo and equipment remaining aboard the F-77.

In the meantime, they wanted to party. There was a passionate new woman in Phil's life. He'd flown a lot around the islands in PAL commercial aircraft, getting to know PAL's office staff. At the booking desk, he kept encountering a voluptuous young Filipina who seemed more feminine than any other. He was not the first to notice. He learned that Nevy Aquino was 25 years old. In her teens her parents had forced her to marry a man they chose, who then died in an accident. Nevy later remarried for love, only to have her second husband killed by Japanese soldiers -- who then took turns raping her. She had survived all this, and was now considering a proposal of marriage from an American commercial pilot named Jim Fleming.

None too subtle, Phil invited the whole PAL office staff to a pool party on his tab at the Manila Hotel.

When everyone brought bathing suits except Nevy, Phil ignored her protests, took her to the hotel boutique and bought her a modest one-piece suit. She looked great in it, darker skinned than Nena Nieto, her black hair tightly curled, with a distinctive Melanesian look about her that was half way between Filipina and Fijian. Phil wondered what his parents would think if he brought her home. There was, he said, "the race question".

Unlike Nena Nieto who was just a good friend, and determined to keep it that way, Nevy Aquino was a serious romance for Phil. She had a college degree as a teacher, and had come to terms with the tragedies in her past, regarding them as simply ancient history. If she married again it would be to have a dozen kids. Meanwhile, if she really liked somebody, sex was full, natural -- as elemental as earth, air, water and fire. Phil was out of his depth, at age 22 still in the process of inventing himself, and in no way ready to make such a profound commitment.

Even so, he was hugely drawn to this very real and passionate woman, but also apprehensive of getting into a deeper romance than he could handle. He confided to Pete that Nevy "gave herself completely to me" yet he remained evasive about what that really meant. But it was evident that he was now in over his head. Unless he made a heavy commitment, Nevy told him she would never date him again, then the following evening she'd again be eager to see him.

He felt he was seriously in love this time – but somebody had to go survey the wrecked F-77 at remote Jomalig Island, to get the insurance.

"The trip was long overdue, nobody else had volunteered, and desperate as we were for funds, we would have serious problems if I did not go. On the other hand, going by road was poor judgment. I had no idea what I was in for."

PAL had flights to many points on the east coast of Luzon, but they were infrequent, so he planned to cross the mountainous spine of Luzon in a JavaChina Jeep, a rough journey that would take him a week or so.

At the Manila Hotel, Phil had been befriended by a Captain Cesar Lucero, a senior officer in the Philippine Military Police in Manila. At the time there seemed nothing odd to Phil about a top policeman introducing himself in such a friendly way. Cheez encouraged Phil to make valuable acquaintances in the hotel. Phil questioned Captain Lucero about how best to get to Jomalig Island. The map showed something called a National Highway to the east coast, but Lucero said that was a gross exaggeration. All it's bridges had been destroyed during the war, and not repaired since; much of it was deeply rutted logging road, with many sections washed-out by typhoons. Lucero volunteered to write a letter to Military Police outposts on the east coast, asking them to lend Phil a small landing craft to reach Jomalig Island. He was not certain which post might have an LCM, so Phil would have to make inquiries when he got there.

Meanwhile, as people were known to disappear in the Sierras, large parts of which were far beyond government control, the captain offered to find Phil two bodyguards with burp guns to go with him.

The trip overland was indeed a nightmare. Even well-traveled stretches were very rough. During monsoon rains, loggers' trucks and bulldozers had mutilated the roadbed. Even with 4-wheel drive, the Jeep got hung up on the deep ruts and had to be dragged or pushed out of the muck by bulldozers, only to spend an hour digging mud out of the radiator before continuing. Where there were jury-rigged bridges, these were logs patched with metal plates or bamboo mat. Small rivers they forded, big rivers they had to wait for rafts to ferry the Jeep across. When they reached a mining town called Paracale, they were joined by a feisty old geezer named Dwyer, an American vet who had stayed in Luzon after the war and married a Filipina.

Dwyer showed Phil how to get to Daet, then Mambulao, where they located a Military Police post that did have an LCM somewhere else -- at a village called Larap on the coast a few more rough miles to the north. The policemen were not about to lend out their LCM, but after

Phil showed them Captain Lucero's letter they agreed reluctantly on the condition that two MPs would go along to protect their boat. Reaching Larap, which was only a collection of Nipa huts, they found the LCM kitted-out like a rustic yacht with a thatched roof over the stern. The local MP post had been radioed to get it ready.

Once Phil's modest supplies were loaded, he left his bodyguards with the Jeep, and he and Dwyer set out with the local MPs to find Jomalig Island and the F-77.

Compared to the butt-breaking Jeep ride, the 35-mile voyage to Pollilio Island and on to Jomalig Island was like a holiday cruise. After skirting their destination warily, they saw the hulk of the F-77 aground on a beach. Off the sandy beach were coral reefs that had torn the hull open as the ship was swept ashore. Her hull now lay askew, bottom deep in sand. Phil took photos of the damage for Lloyds. At high tide, waves lapped at her stern and hid numerous hazards. Mounted on the stern was a small hoist they could use to transfer everything of value to the LCM. The F-77's crew was long gone to the mainland, and most cargo had been pilfered. But they did salvage a Harley-Davidson motorcycle and stripped all the remaining equipment that had been too large or heavy for others to carry away easily.

Once the LCM was fully loaded, they tried to back away, but its props got tangled in lines the crew had rigged after she went aground. As the crippled F-77 had settled into the sand, the lines had sagged and become hidden by sand. To get the LCM free, they had to wait for low tide to untangle the props. When that was done, their batteries were dead. It was not Phil's day.

For a week they were stranded on Jomalig, out of food and forced to accept bony fish, 'pagong' turtle eggs, and 'camote' sweet-potato gruel from a village of friendly negrito fishing folk who were the island's only inhabitants.

In return, they shot a small wild boar that they shared with the villagers. One of the negritos had a homemade 'proa' dugout with a small triangular sail, and was willing to take Phil and Dwyer back to Larap for help. Leaving the MPs behind with the loaded LCM, they sailed the dugout for ten hours through choppy seas, arriving at Larap exhausted and soaked. The MPs at Larap gave the courageous negrito a portable battery charger to take back to the stranded LCM, which he did next morning.

Eager to see Nevy, Phil hitched a ride to Daet where he could get a plane to Manila. He left Dwyer with the Jeep and instructions to sell the salvaged goods for whatever he could get -- except for the Harley, which Phil later had shipped to Manila.

"I was still in seventh-heaven about Nevy, and could not wait to get back—but my trip gave her the time to regain her senses, and do the smart thing: agreeing to marry Jim Fleming.

"It was the first time I was dumped!"

Phil Mehan at 12 with sister Peggy and brother Ralph

To advance his career in Counter-Intelligence, Edward G. Lansdale, was determined to prove that Phil was part of a Soviet spy ring in Manila.

Phil Mehan, age 22, with his first moustache, while being tracked by Lansdale and his intelligence officers.

Phil, earlier, as a raw U.S. Army recruit

Phil as a proud young Merchant Mariner

Gun-happy engineer 'Pete' Peterson in khakis.
He persuaded Phil to work for Java-China.

When 'Cheez' (left) arrived in Manila, he splurged on this Cadillac with Java-China funds.

Phil at the wheel of a Java-China jeep.

When Cheez got them a suite at the Manila Hotel,
Phil met Nena Nieto (left) and her friend 'Babs'.

Phil's first true love, Nevy Aquino (third from left),
jilted him.

Always dashing Peterson with "Babs" and Nena Nieto.

World War Two vet Dwyer (far left) guided
Phil to Jomalig Island.

The F-77 wrecked on Jomalig Island.

Phil's loggers made supper of the lizard he caught.

Pete escaped prison when he quit Java-China and fled to
Shanghai, where he married to his girlfriend Kitty.

Cheez rented this new house on Roberts Road.

Cheez's wife Nina and son Georgie, were expelled to China.

Cheez clowns with Dorothy Goebbels .

Phil and Cheez's logging operation at pretty Iman point.

Phil's pal and new partner, canny Jerry Widrin.

Phil and Widrin planned to escape to Borneo on this LCM

Tied up in the Pasig River, the LCM was stormed by police.

Phil and Widrin were both held at Bilibad Prison. Plain outside, inside it was a cesspit.

Phil escaped the Manila police on this motorcycle.

Safe in the USA, Phil met and married Iris-Marie.

A happy ending, and a new family.

Chapter 14 :

GOING BROKE

While Phil was stranded on Jomalig Island, Cheez set out for Baler where one of the two PT-boats lost by the F-93 in Typhoon Opal was reported washed up on a beach. Not fond of hardship, he simply bought a round-trip airline ticket and flew to Baler in comfort. After inspecting the PT-boat, which had a big hole in it, he visited the mayor of Baler and through him hired local people to recover the diesel engine, a 5 KW generator, and an outboard motor. He gave the outboard motor to the mayor by way of thanks. Then, being a gregarious and expansive man, Cheez threw a big party with door prizes of 50 pesos to each Baler girl who showed up -- a good week's wages for them. Until recently, Cheez's life had been cold, hard, lonely, and hungry. An avid reader of novels and short stories, his role models were the doomed romantics of Conrad and Dostoevsky, who hoped that luck or karma would come to their rescue, but knew all along it would not. JavaChina had changed his life. Cheez had arrived in Manila in June 1946 with $180,000 of JavaChina's U.S. dollars in large denomination bills in his shoes. For several months thereafter, lots more money arrived from JavaChina by other discreet channels.

Still further sums were made available to him through the Manila Branch of a Dutch East Indies bank called Nederlandische Indische Handelsbank NV. This all came to a grand total of nearly a quarter of a million U.S. Dollars -- enough in those days to turn anyone's head. For the next six months, he lived as though the well would never run dry, knowing all along that it would.

Sharing the suite with him at the Manila Hotel, Phil had been amazed and appalled at how Cheez threw money around, often taking it out to count, fondle, or make sure it was real. Seeing him do that, the eyes of room-service boys got big. Cheez could also not resist flashing fat rolls of bills in the hotel lobby. So everybody working in the hotel was accustomed to seeing the gregarious Russian guy being extravagant. When Phil was in Manila, his being a teetotaler restrained Cheez, and kept him from being too extravagant. When Phil was away, Cheez reverted to his garrulous habits. At drinking parties in their suite, where

Phil drank only sodas, he cringed when Cheez bellowed to all the girls: "Enough foreplay, let's make love!"

Trained well by his parents, Phil knew he was spending 175 pesos (about $90) a day: 25 pesos for his share of the suite, 25 pesos for food, 100 for taxis, and 25 for incidentals. Phil and Pete's original JavaChina deal guaranteed living expenses of $300 each per month. Cheez was spending up to $300 each day. At that rate, from June to December, some $45,000 mostly on the suite, dining well, and throwing parties.

Granted, this was all part of the plan to make JavaChina look good, make powerful friends, and in that way expedite repairs to the ships. To be sure, some went to foolish luxuries. In the past, Phil and Pete had commuted to Cavite shipyard on two Army surplus motorcycles. Cheez could not see himself riding a motorcycle, so he purchased several surplus U.S. Army Jeeps, then had them converted into Jitneys with a roof because of all the rain, and repainted with the JavaChina logo stenciled below the windshields. Then he decided it was better for his image to have something flashier. For 11,000 pesos ($5,000 plus change) he bought a 1941 Cadillac sedan, one of only two in the country. He was stung: It was not in good shape, the transmission seized, and the Cadillac spent the next few months up on blocks awaiting a buyer.

Cheez was now caught in a squeeze. He had been sent to The Philippines to rescue JavaChina from a predicament of its own making, and given a great deal of money to do so. Now he was being pressed by JavaChina for an accounting. When you are told to solve a problem by throwing money at it, you may find it difficult later to justify what was done.

Aside from equipping the original five F-boats with things the U.S. Army had failed to provide, which had to be purchased on the blackmarket, there had been many unanticipated costs: for emergency ship repairs, endless bribes, advance payments to the Seamen's Union, wages to captains and crews, the purchase of two additional F-Boats, the PT-boats, and the luxurious Crash Boat -- all things Winkelman demanded.

Cheez was not an accountant. He had kept hasty notations on scraps of paper, paper napkins, and stuffed receipts into his pocket to sort out later. Eventually, he had passed these rough accounts to Shanghai.

Counting money one day during Phil's absence at Jomalig Island, Cheez saw he was even running low on what he considered petty cash.

He felt a spasm of anguish because his wife and son were about to arrive from Shanghai. He needed a fast way to replenish the company purse. With a snoot full of vodka, he took a taxi to "Ye Olde Mansion", one of Harry Stonehill's gambling establishments, on General Solano Street. By closing time he had lost 35,000 pesos, nearly $18,000. That hurt.

Ever since he had left Shanghai in June 1946, he had been obsessed with getting his entire family out of China -- not only Nina and Georgie, but her aging parents. Part of getting resettled in The Philippines had been to make a big impression on wealthy and powerful people. Cheez and Winkelman had discussed setting up a business in the islands, like shipping frozen fish to Manila from the out-islands. His family would then be secure. This was the fuel of his fantasy.

Through a friend who was the agriculture attache at the U.S. Embassy in Manila, Cheez had obtained a six-month visa for Nina and Georgie. A radiogram had been sent to the U.S. Consulate in Shanghai authorizing issuance of the visa. Cheez was assured that it would be easy to get the visa extended once his wife and son were in The Philippines. Anything could be done by a bribe to officials running the immigration racket.

Unfortunately, Nina -- like Cheez -- had only a Russian passport, issued in Shanghai after the Japanese surrender, by the Consulate of the Soviet Union. No matter what your political views, if you were a Russian and needed travel documents, you had few choices. So when Nina went to the U.S. Consulate to have the visa stamped in her passport, the American clerks froze -- staring at her passport as if it was a cobra. All Nina got was double-talk. Everyone in the Consulate had arrived recently from the United States, and reflected new attitudes in Washington, which was in the grip of a growing postwar anti-communist panic. Nobody wanted to hear about White Russians being different from Red Russians. The U.S. Consul gave Nina the brush-off, lying to her that she could get the six-month visa stamped in her passport once she got to Manila.

Instead, drowsy Immigration officers at Manila Airport stamped in a usual 30-day tourist visa. Her days in Paradise, and Georgie's, were to be numbered.

Pushing all that out of mind, Nina and Georgie moved in with Cheez at the Manila Hotel suite. From that moment on, Cheez was a changed man, no longer the wild man from Siberia. He was genuinely in love with Nina, and adored his son, for good reason.

In her mid-twenties, Nina was a pretty blonde, with deep blue eyes and lots of freckles. Because she was slim and small, only five feet two, she wore high-heels all the time, and gauzy dresses that showed off her figure. A photo shows a sweet young mother with a clear gaze, innocent of guile, a protective hand on the shoulder her little boy.

She made sure Georgie was always neatly dressed in shorts, starched white shirts, had a fresh handkerchief in his pocket, and his white socks were neatly turned down at the ankles, above chunky brown leather shoes.

Even so, there were things pushed out of mind that caused Nina to bite her nails. She felt certain that she and Georgie were being watched each time they left the Manila Hotel for a walk in the park or along the bayfront. When the phone rang, she thought she heard a tell-tale click in the background, with someone listening in. Maids showed up three times a day to empty the suite's small trash baskets, when there was nothing in them. She didn't talk about this with Cheez until one day, when a letter from her mother in Shanghai arrived at the suite already opened. Nina burst into tears.

Blithely, Cheez carried on as if there were no problems. Their household now included a sweet faced 23-year-old Filipina hired as a nursemaid for Georgie. In Shanghai Nina always had a girl to help with Georgie, and Cheez did not want to disappoint her now. To give them more privacy, Phil moved into another room at the Manila Hotel. They took Phil and one of his girlfriends, Dorothy Goebbels, on a picnic. The picnic was to cheer Cheez up.

He was increasingly worried, being relentlessly pressed by Winkelman to account for every penny he had spent. Winkelman was making these demands in a hostile and menacing way.

In truth, the whole affair of ship purchases was badly managed by Hertzka, Samet, and Winkelman.

They had squandered hundreds of thousands of dollars, without paying close attention, then blamed everything on Phil, Pete and Cheez, their new employees. Winkelman had been so obsessed about getting his money out of Shanghai before the roof caved in, that he had handed over great sums in cash to Hertzka, to Samet, to Cheez, to Nina, and anyone else who happened to be heading to Manila. Accustomed to doing so, Winkelman would have been hard-pressed to produce satisfactory documents of his own transactions. Even the basic contract for the F-boats had been signed in blank.

Now Phil was being pressed by Winkelman to justify Cheez's accounts, or share the blame. It was in their mutual interest to square things with Winkelman, because both Phil and Cheez had outstanding wages to collect. Since Cheez was now playing host to Nina and Georgie, Phil gathered all the documents he could find, and flew to Shanghai to go over accounts with Dr. Samet.

According to Phil's own review, JavaChina's Manila operation now had assets of 22,000 pesos, against outstanding debts of 30,000 pesos. JavaChina insisted that Manila's outstanding debts were closer to 50,000 pesos. So by Winkelman's reckoning, some 30,000 pesos had gone missing. Samet seemed kindly and sympathetic, but Winkelman was in a snit and went on the attack:

"The results of five years of damned hard work have been squandered by a handful of irresponsible youngsters."

Grudgingly, Winkelman conceded that Phil and Cheez did have legitimate claims for several months of unpaid wages, and legitimate expenses, but he challenged many disparities in their accounts. Phil counter-attacked that he and Pete had signed on only to oversee the U.S. Army's repairs to the F-boats, and then to move the vessels to Shanghai, which they did in the face of endless delays and obstructions by the U.S. Army and the Seamen's Union, plus outright sabotage by the hired Filipino captains.

Phil rubbed Winkelman's nose in the ugly fact that Felix Hertzka had bungled the deal from the outset by signing blank contracts. This allowed the Army to fob off its worst vessels, and to drag out the refitting over so many months that JavaChina had to pay stiff penalties to its clients, without the Army paying any penalties at all. Meanwhile, Phil, Pete and Cheez had been forced to scrounge for missing equipment on the blackmarket, and pay out of pocket. As to Cheez, he had been chosen by Winkelman, given a huge sum, and sent to Manila to spend the money 'expediting' (whatever that involved), to make JavaChina look good. Neither Phil nor Pete could be held to account for Cheez's behavior, or his spending habits.

But even allowing for extravagance, and specific instances of stupidity, such as buying the Cadillac, most of Cheez's expenditures were to do Winkelman's bidding:

Salaries for Cheez, Pete and Phil totaled $10,000. Provisioning a single crew for a delivery ran $500 a week; because of delays and disasters, Cheez had to spend more than $5,000 on food for crews.

Tens of thousands of gallons of diesel also had to be purchased. These fuel costs were doubled by storms, delays and mischief. They were swindled of $5,500 by MadDog Mabini at the Seaman's Union. Thereafter Phil was obliged to hire non-union crews and foreign captains, for another $10,000. There were $100 bribes to greedy Army officers and port officials, for another $2,000. When promised equipment was not provided by the U.S. Army, those items had to be purchased on the blackmarket for $18,000. There were many fines paid to Philippine maritime authorities, starting with $2,500 for the mischief of Captain Dimuahuan. Then, when Winkelman made new demands, Cheez paid for six PT-boats at $2,000 a piece, and two LCMs for the same amount, totaling $16,000. Buying the elegant crash-boat cost nearly $15,000. The two additional F-Boats cost $60,000. JavaChina also ordered them to find and purchase surplus equipment and other goods to place aboard the ships during delivery, for resale in Shanghai. This came to another $15,000. Five Jeeps were purchased for $3,000 and converted into Jeepneys. Several motorcycles were bought at $210 apiece. The Cadillac cost $5,000. Since time pressure was severe, many trips were made by plane, totaling some $3,000. Just off the top of one's head, this came to roughly $180-thousand. That, plus hotel suite and living expenses for six months, covered virtually all that Cheez had spent. He seemed careless in manner, but in fact was not.

That being the case, Winkelman was unfairly making them scapegoats. Phil told Winkelman he was damned lucky he had been in America when Pete arrived in Shanghai with his two magnums. Pete had been in no mood to just shoot out lights. Winkelman's knees had been his targets of choice.

The Dutchman could not admit his own guilt. Even as he raged at Phil and Cheez, he still toyed with the idea of "expanding my investments in The Philippines", continuing to seek proposals from Cheez and Phil for a possible ship-repair facility, transport of cargos like frozen fish or copra, or logging and hauling mahogany hardwoods to the big Manila market.

Suspecting that Winkelman was losing his mind, Phil argued that everything could be resolved if JavaChina swapped its remaining assets in Manila for the overdue pay to Phil and Cheez. Also, he said, JavaChina would have to assume the burden of resolving the Seamen's Union claim for back-wages, or fighting it in court. That was a company problem. He and Cheez were only employees, doing the company's bidding. Other outstanding but relatively small company debts in Manila would be settled by Cheez and Phil through the sale of the Cadillac, Jeeps, and other odds and ends.

"It seemed a fair exchange, since it would allow JavaChina to liquidate their equipment at a profit while providing assets for Cheez and me to proceed immediately in a new enterprise."

The assets they would acquire from JavaChina included the Cadillac, a Jeep, an LCM, two surviving PT-boats, miscellaneous furniture and equipment, and 4,000 pesos in cash.

Since JavaChina expected to receive full payment from Lloyd's of London for the F-77, and Phil had already recovered and sold all he could recover from that wreck, the company would recover full value of the crippled F-boat. Winkelman agreed. Phil returned to Manila.

While Phil was gone, Cheez himself had drastically cut expenses by $700 a month by moving his wife and son, and their nanny, out of the Manila Hotel suite to an unfurnished house at 321 Roberts Road, near the Merchant Seamen's Club on bayside Dewey Boulevard. Two young Filipinas were hired for a pittance to clean and do laundry under the nanny's supervision.

To furnish the rented house, Cheez bought a simple electric stove, a cheap refrigerator, and inexpensive, locally-made rattan furniture.

The house on Roberts Road was brand new and attractive. They were its first occupants. It was a single-level ranch style house, built neatly of block and stucco. Floors were polished local hardwood. The windows were barred against thieves, which made Nina feel safe when Cheez was away working. Nina's security worried Cheez; she was pretty, and did not speak a word of Tagalog.

There were three bedrooms and modern plumbing: bathtub, shower, sinks, toilets. There was a shaded porch, and striped canvas awnings over the windows. Inside, the house was cooled by ceiling fans. The garden wasn't big, but gave Georgie a place to play jacks on the cement terrace. Laundry lines were neatly strung in the back garden.

Finding such a house in Manila those days was like discovering gold. It was part of a new development reserved for civilian employees of the War Liquidation Commission and high-ranking politicians or visiting consultants. To rent one required connections. The man who made it possible for Cheez was Captain Cesar Lucero, of the Philippine Military Police, reporting directly to Malacañang Palace, and by extension part of Lansdale's G-2 operation. Lucero had approached Phil and Cheez in the lobby of the Manila Hotel, introduced himself, and became a fast friend. It was Lucero who helped Phil get to Jomalig Island, providing two bodyguards to accompany him cross-country, and two MPs to man the LCM that took him to Jomalig. Was he only being generous?

G-2 had been watching Cheez closely for seven months since June 13 when he first stepped off the plane from Shanghai. They tailed Cheez to Cavite where he introduced himself to Phil and Pete. From that moment on, G-2 agents had also watched every move of Phil and Pete. Not one day passed without men watching them. In the Manila Hotel, G-2 had eager cooperation from Colonel Nieto, so all the hotel staff was instructed to report on who went to their suite, what happened in the suite, noting their comings and goings, monitoring their phone calls, opening all their mail, copying their radiograms. The front desk reported every transaction. When G-2 snoops got wind of Cheez's financial predicament, Captain Lucero was told to arrange the Roberts Road house, practically next door to Lucero's own home.

This way, the White Russian family, and all who came to see them, would be under convenient surveillance by Lucero, his wife, or intelligence agents posing as gardeners, fruit vendors, or street cleaners.

Cheez was so accustomed to drawing attention that he paid no mind to being watched. He thought they were immigration agents. He thought it was comic that people were so frightened of Russians. How could anyone be so ignorant? If they had offered him a job reporting on all the White Russian emigres working in Manila, or just passing through, he would have been delighted. But nobody asked. Of all the people he had met, Cheez thought Captain Lucero was one of the Good Guys. As it turned out, Cheez was half-right. With Lucero as a proximate neighbor, Cheez felt better about the security of his family. He liked Lucero. What better security from mischief-makers than to be next-door neighbors with a chief of Military Police?

What Cheez never guessed was that the danger to his life came not from smalltime punks, but from Grand Inquisitors and their professional thugs, who were about to pounce.

Chapter 15 :

THE BIGGER PICTURE

Christmas 1946 was approaching when Phil moved in with Cheez and Nina at the Roberts Road house, on his return from haggling with Winkelman in Shanghai. He found a pleasant family atmosphere: Nina was pleased to be with Cheez, and Georgie was ecstatic to be with his daddy and Uncle Phil. They were not expecting the Spanish Inquisition.

Phil spent most of December liquidating JavaChina property, trying with Cheez to negotiate more favorable terms with company creditors. Complaints about these unpaid debts were getting noisy. Every time the two young men returned to Roberts Road they found creditors loitering on the front porch. When Cheez pleaded for time, they gestured at the Cadillac still on blocks in the driveway as proof that they could pay now. Without a transmission, the Cadillac was a white elephant; no Cadillac replacement was available, and they had not yet considered installing a Chevrolet gear box from the same manufacturer. Only then could it be sold.

Cheez ignored the creditors, and sent out invitations to a big Christmas party on December 26. On the morning of the party, returning home with cartons of booze and snacks, they found Nina in tears. She ran to Cheez and threw her arms around his neck, crying out in Russian.

Two detectives from the Manila Police Department (MPD) were waiting in the living room. Nina was certain these were men she had seen before, lurking around or tailing her. Now, they had bullied their way into the house, following Nina from room to room, asking questions and making threats. She was terrified by how much the policemen knew about her, her husband, their lives back in Shanghai.

In the living room, Cheez and Phil saw a tall thin Filipino in a rumpled suit, sitting on the floor, legs splayed, playing jacks with Georgie. The other detective was short and stocky. Phil snapped at them: "I'm Captain Mehan, what can I do for you?" The short one handed Phil a card identifying him as Detective Sergeant Crispiano Carlos.

"We are agents of the Philippine Government. For the past seven months, we have been investigating Mr. Chirskoff and his family, as well as you and your partner, Mr. Peterson. From things we have uncovered we believe you are all in the pay of communists."

Nina collapsed in Cheez's arms.

"Whatever gave you that crazy idea?" Phil asked. "Many things," replied Carlos, smirking. This was his moment.

Carlos recounted that since Cheez's arrival at Manila Airport on June 13th they had been the targets of a major investigation by American and Filipino counter-intelligence services.

Being told is one thing. Comprehending is another.

Both Phil and Cheez were shaking their heads in disbelief.

Detective Carlos again blurted out the bizarre allegation that they were Soviet agents.

They had wondered many times why there had been so many delays, obstacles, and outright mischief blocking their efforts to make the F-boats seaworthy and deliver them to China, and why the Seamen's Union in particular caused them so much grief. Now a possible explanation was dawning on them.

Still, they simply did not grasp or understand The Bigger Picture.

In the few months since the end of World War II, the great tide against fascism had crested and subsided, replaced by a reverse tide against the successful enemies of fascism. With it came an undertow of Inquisition, in which any disagreeable or inconvenient heretic could be labeled a communist or leftist, or at least a Fellow Traveller, which was enough to destroy a career.

In Asia this was resulting in the purge of distinguished U.S. diplomats like John Service, who were critical of the corrupt Nationalist Chinese dictator Generalissimo Chiang Kai-shek. But to imagine Cheez, Pete, or Phil as communists was wildly implausible on the face of it.

They were simply too naive and incompetent to be spies or secret agents for anyone -- right or left. Yet the 'facts' and juiced-up speculations about them are documented word-for-word in the Project Manila dossier, Philippine legal records, and witness interviews. With the dogged tenacity of Dominican medieval inquisitors, the witch-hunt focused on the misadventures of three men without guile and a hapless young mother, all still in their twenties and wet behind the ears.

Why would such an intense investigation unfold, involving hundreds of hours of labor by agents, generating thousands of pages of reports and analyses, to mildew for decades in top secret files before being laundered, declassified, and sent to the U.S. National Archives? The answer lies not too well hidden in the term: counter-intelligence.

This surveillance was conducted not only by law enforcement, secret services, and G-2 in Manila, but in Shanghai, Tokyo, and the United States. In Manila and Tokyo, all these agents were under the control of General MacArthur's 'amiable fascist' General Charles Willoughby, his deputy in Manila G-2, Colonel Joseph McMicking, and Major Lansdale. On the ground, the spear-carriers were led by the not-too-bright detective Carlos, under the direct supervision of Captain Cesar Lucero of the Military Police Command, who had cleverly arranged to be their neighbor. Not one of them suspected Lucero, who seemed discreet, helpful, and sympathetic. Mrs. Lucero was a charming matron who gave Nina advice about living in The Philippines; she sent toys to Georgie, and listened patiently to Nina's worries. Nina and Cheez thought it was lucky to have the Luceros for friends.

They did not know that Lucero's Military Police (another name for the Philippine Constabulary), was intimately tied to Lansdale and the U.S. Counter-Intelligence Corps, the Manila Police Secret Service, the Malacañang Palace Secret Service, the Manila Harbor Secret Service, the Immigration Bureau, and the National Bureau of Investigation -- all of them watching Cheez, Pete, Phil, Nina and Georgie.

Detective Carlos on the other hand was unable to keep secrets, or to hide his swagger. He liked intimidating people, working the stick, instead of the carrot. So, after terrifying Nina that morning, he blurted out to Phil and Cheez that he had a fat file on everything they had done the past seven months. When the two detectives left for lunch that morning of the Christmas Party, Carlos ordered Phil and Cheez to show up at police headquarters at 4pm that afternoon, for formal interrogation.

Phil made sure they got to Carlos's office well in advance. Carlos had his desk in what was recklessly called the Intelligence Unit.

Before questioning them, Carlos picked up from his desk and waved at Phil and Cheez his copy of the six-inch thick G-2 dossier.

It was chock full of intercepted mail, cables, transcripts of phone conversations, copied bank records, interviews with Manila Hotel clerks, bar tenders, barbers, restauranteurs, jitney drivers, and a few jealous or jilted girlfriends.

According to the dossier, from the moment Cheez had stepped off the plane from Shanghai with a Soviet passport on June 13, 1946, Immigration had alerted all police that "a suspected Russian communist agent" had entered The Philippines.

At a time when thousands of refugees and displaced persons were milling around Asia, using Manila as a transit turnstile, they were sure this one was a secret agent because he had a Soviet passport. That instantly upgraded the threat from orange to red, turning suspicion into fact.

When Cheez went immediately to Cavite harbor to introduce himself to Phil and Pete, more alarms sounded, and the two Americans also became "probable Soviet agents". Within days, Cheez had installed Phil in the Manila Hotel with him, to be joined later by Pete, so the entire hotel staff were put on alert that there was a Soviet cell in one of their suites.

As the manager, Colonel Nieto, was a member of MacArthur's inner circle, friend of the "amiable fascist" General Willoughby, the super-rich Colonel McMicking who was married into the San Miguel Beer family, and a crony of Vice President Quirino, Nieto had taken an immediate personal interest in Cheez and Phil.

Hence his extreme dislike of Phil's goofing-off beside the pool, and Phil's antics in entering the dining room in his brief bathingsuit. For this to be done by a California brat was bad enough, but for the brat also to be a Soviet agent caused nitro-glycerine to flood Nieto's veins and arteries. All it took for Nieto to fly into an uncontrolled rage was to have his defiant daughter Nena side with the young lout. Revenge merged with anticommunist zeal.

After that, Phil was a marked man, his every move watched with interest, around the pool and on the dance floor.

In Shanghai, official heavy-breathing was provoked by Phil's delivery of the PEONY while traveling without a proper Philippine exit permit.

G-2 in China cabled G-2 in Manila: "F-92 arrived in Shanghai 9 OCT 46 under command of Philip A. Mehan, former seaman in US

126

Army Transportation Corps. Cargo of ship is being examined. Mehan left this morning by plane for Manila, to be followed without arousing suspicion."

These reports went directly to Lansdale, with a copy to Malacañang Palace secret service.

After waving around the fat dossier, their interviews by Detective Carlos that afternoon were conducted in front of a stenographer. As recorded in the Project Manila dossier, both young men were frank and up-front.

Cheez was questioned first. He understood tyranny, hid his contempt for institutionalized stupidity, and was careful what he told Detective Carlos and others who interrogated him later. He stuck to the facts. He did not deny he had expressed 'opinions' about man's inhumanity to man, not that his opinion mattered, or was in any way radical. But in Manila, where inhumanity was the norm, this sounded alarmingly Leftist.

Phil did not give opinions. He related events as he recalled them. In the dossier, his statements are apolitical. The only time he had made a political comment was in a letter to his parents observing that postwar America was facing economic turmoil with a normal postwar downturn. Raised by hard-working, church-going Americans, who had headed West during the Great Depression to improve their lives in California, his views followed cherished traditions of Puritan capitalism, spiced with humor. Phil would have been at home with Benjamin Franklin.

Phil and Cheez were tense, not knowing where this would lead. They almost burst out laughing when Carlos showed them "the incriminating evidence" -- a letter addressed to the Provost Marshal in Manila. It was headed 'Communist Activities'.

The letter stated that Cheez, Phil and Pete were hiring expensive taxis and had purchased a 1942 Cadillac sedan for 11,000 pesos. Cheez said the information about the taxis and the Cadillac was correct, but they had spent far greater sums on ship repairs and crews, yet the letter deemed a malfunctioning Cadillac 'irregular'. Carlos dropped the Cadillac and asked a question no interrogator would ever ask a spy: "Do you intend to make The Philippines your home?"

Cheez: If I am treated fairly and not subjected to the sort of treatment which I have been getting from the authorities lately, I shall stay here and go into the fishing business. If I continue to be constantly pushed around, I will leave.

Carlos: What is the source of your funds?

Cheez: JavaChina Trading Company.

Carlos: Did you actually pay so much for the Cadillac?

Cheez: Yes, it was cheap at the time.

Carlos: Are you a Russian?

Cheez: Yes.

Carlos: Do you belong to a political party?

Cheez: No.

Carlos: Why are you so inconsistent? How can you be a Russian and not belong to a political party?

Cheez: That is not inconsistent. I have not been in Russian territory since I was a small child, and only acquired a Soviet passport recently [to travel to Manila from Shanghai]. My parents were White Russians [anti-communist], and therefore I am stateless. I belong to no party and have no political convictions.

Carlos: When did you leave Russia?

Cheez: When I was eight and one-half years old.

Stymied in this line of questions, Carlos pulled out a list boldly labelled: 'MEETING PLACES OF SPIES'. Cheez said he had only been to one, and only when he met Captain Lucero there. Why did being at a "meeting place of spies" not cast doubt on Lucero.

Carlos: Who is Mehan?

Cheez: Mehan is an American citizen employed by JavaChina.

Cheez: We had plenty of money when we first began operations here, but it was company money advanced from [JavaChina] to pay our living and business expenses. Most of the money was used overhauling freighters the company purchased. ... Look, your people profited from the money we spent, and from the salaries we paid... Now we are broke -- [JavaChina] ran out of money with all the problems we had getting the ships ready. That is why we're living in a small rented cottage. All that can be said about our having money is, it proves we are capitalists, not communists."

Carlos (turning palms up sheepishly): "You are broke then?"

Cheez: "Completely, and that's not all, we're fifty thousand pesos in debt. If you were such a good investigator, you would already know that."

. . .

Stirred, but not shaken, Cheez and Phil went home to make final preparations for their Christmas party.

They had learned more from Carlos about the G-2 surveillance than Carlos had learned about them.

Was their greatest sin being rich for a while, or being in debt, and which of these proved you were a Communist. It was surreal.

Surreal things were happening all over Asia, nowhere stranger than in Tokyo, where General MacArthur, General Bonner Fellers, and former U.S. President Herbert Hoover were busy rescuing Emperor Hirohito and the Imperial Family from shame, and putting Japan back in the hands of the same fanatics America and its Allies had just defeated. General Willoughby was personally in charge of exonerating Japan's most notorious war criminals, liberating them from Sugamo Prison, giving them covert employment with what would be the new CIA. Among them were underworld godfather Yoshio Kodama. Washington was persuaded that only Japan's fascists were sufficiently anti-Communist to stop the red tide in Asia.

Common sense should have made it clear that Cheez and his parents were refugees from the Bolshevik Terror, and that Cheez came to Manila hoping to set up a secure home for his wife and son before China fell to Mao. Anyone bothering to check the record could see he was now escaping before the inevitable Red Chinese regime: escaping communism, not embracing it. Cheez made this point repeatedly, but Interrogators are only promoted if they prove more anti-Satan than the Pope.

Their personal agendas and pathology denied what was obvious, and they searched for evidence of what was not. Lansdale told Bohannan explicitly: "I have the charges, you invent the facts!"

Lansdale's office circulated top secret memos declaring that they had 'provocative' evidence that Cheez and his associates had been sent to encourage and arm the Huks, with the objective of overthrowing the government of The Philippines. Urged on by Lansdale, the G-2 file shows that Colonel Nieto gave his assistant managers, bartenders, waiters, room-boys, and laundry-ladies, instructions to report everything done or said by Phil, Pete, or Cheez, while reading their mail, searching their rooms and wastebaskets, listening to their phone calls at the switchboard. Copies were sent to U.S. Embassies and Consulates across East Asia, to the Shanghai Municipal Police, to the Office of Naval Intelligence (ONI) in Washington. In Manila, the Bureau of Labor was ordered to investigate JavaChina's 'swindle' of Filipino mariners, while Mabini at the Seamen's Union prepared a lawsuit for 'Estafa' -- the fraudulent non-payment of wages. Countless man-hours were invested in trying to get evidence, however circumstantial.

There were careers to be boosted, great sums to be misappropriated by the U.S. Congress for the new anti-communist crusade. As Lansdale pointed out many times, this was best done by stirring the pot, and scaring everyone.

"If there isn't fire," he told Bohannan, "we'll light one." If the Huks were not sufficiently 'marxist' or sufficiently 'terrorist', Lansdale and his men would and did stage all the acts of terror needed, using special units of the Philippine Army pretending to be Huks, while Lansdale's movie cameras filmed the attacks.

But to get evidence that the Huks were actively being encouraged, financed, and armed by the Kremlin, Lansdale needed a 'smoking gun' -- an actual Soviet agent caught red-handed in The Philippines.

As Cheez and Phil were being morphed from Loose Cannons into Soviet Agents, the anticommunist careers of President Roxas and Vice-President Quirino were flourishing. Both men had served in the Japanese wartime government and were widely regarded as collaborators who should have been tried after the war, or prohibited from ever again holding public office. Instead, General MacArthur made sure 'his boys' were exonerated.

· · ·

At the Christmas Party on Roberts Road that night in December 1946, most of the guests were either agents or informers. Captain Lucero and his wife were there, along with the Mayor and Secretary of the town of Baler, in Quezon Province, to whom Cheez had given an outboard motor, and $25 each to all the local girls present, clear evidence of undercover activities.

Tracking events at the party, G-2 reports said the Baler officials were "on the most intimate and friendly terms with Chirskoff, and had brought him three cases that he had left behind in Baler, which ... only contained dresses, cosmetics, and other personal articles [for] his wife [Nina]". Hoping to find guns or seditious political tracts, G-2 had gone through the trunks, only to draw a blank.

They concluded that Cheez had attempted to 'subvert' the Mayor of Baler with gifts, enlisting him in the communist conspiracy.

A party informant had instructions to extract information about Peterson from Phil: "[Phil] said Peterson was in Shanghai, a quarrelsome type when drinking, and slightly 'gun happy'. [Phil] stated that when Peterson had been drinking, the slightest argument would cause him to whip out a revolver and threaten to shoot the other individual involved." Peterson, the informant said, had shot up several bars in Shanghai, pulled his revolver on a traffic cop, and later on a union official. Clear evidence of Pete's temper, but not his politics.

To be sure, many men in Manila carried a gun, licensed or otherwise. Before guns, they carried blowpipes and poison-tipped darts, bows and arrows.

The informers took careful note of all ladies at the party, reporting that Phil was "escorting Dorothy May Goebbels of the War Damage Commission."

Phil knew Cheez was short of cash, but he did not know that Cheez had gambled away some of JavaChina's assets at a casino. G-2 agents knew every detail.

After the Christmas party, the scope of Project Manila was expanded because of 'mounting evidence'.

Captain Lucero interrogated Cheez's acquaintance in the local plywood business, Maximilian Zalevsky, who had once lent Cheez 5,000 pesos (some agent reports inflated this to five thousand dollars). Lucero's report was detailed:

"ZALEVSKY, Maximilian is about 6'2", 190 lbs., well-built, blond hair, round face -- a "snappy" dresser, very talkative, speaks four languages. Born in Vladivostok but left at age 4 when Bolsheviks came there, lived in Shanghai, then came to Manila just before World War Two. Says his family were Russian aristocracy opposed to the Bolsheviks. [Elsewhere G-2 says they were Polish, although they could have been Russians of Polish derivation.] Says his father is with a shipping firm in Shanghai. Zalevsky is manager of Findlay Lumber Co. in Manila. With regard to Chirskoff, Zalevsky states that Chirskoff is a poor businessman, who bought ships that needed too many expensive repairs, and owes Zalevsky money. Says Chirskoff has 'considerable communistic tendencies'."

Another informant was Robert Buda, a jeweler from Shanghai, who had passed through Manila on his way to resettle in the United States. Buda was one of the 'mules' who had smuggled JavaChina dollars out of Shanghai to Manila. So he was targeted by G-2 as part of Cheez's greater 'communist' ring. In fact, Buda was a former employee of JavaChina. He had made a personal loan of 5,000 pesos to Cheez that was not repaid because JavaChina's well had run dry. The fact that Buda and Zalevsky each had a personal grudge against Cheez, having lent him money, was not seen by G-2 as invalidating the inflammatory statements they made about Cheez having radical views. Nor did G-2 acknowledge that Buda would say whatever he thought they wanted to hear, to protect his status in the Philippines.

Nobody was weighing evidence in terms of right or wrong, only in terms of right or left. In the end G-2 wanted only to draw conclusions supporting Lansdale's wildly exaggerated anti-communist agenda. Because of his warm relations with Cheez and Phil, Lucero played a curious double role as G-2 point man. Personally, Lucero seemed to have no axe to grind, but as a professional policeman his career depended on results. He repeatedly told G-2 that Cheez was "probably a Communist agent" and this ultimately helped doom his friend. Whatever his real opinions were, he kept them to himself. This is curious because Lucero knew everything, and was a smart man.

Once when Cheez had been celebrating his twenty-ninth birthday at the bar in the Manila Hotel, he told Lucero his entire history, which the captain transcribed afterward. The details are not different in any way from Cheez's depositions to investigators: "I was born on Oct. 31st, 1917, in Vladivostok, Siberia. [In 1926] I left Vladivostok with my parents ... and we went to Beppu, Japan, with the hope that the hot springs there would improve my mother's arthritis... Later we moved to Yokohama where I was educated at St. Joseph's College. After graduation I had jobs with various foreign firms in Tokyo and Yokohama. In August 1940, I left for Shanghai, then brought over my parents in November of the same year. In Shanghai I was associated with ship and repair work until WW2.

"I have a great many friends of various nationalities.

"Upon liberation, I took work with JavaChina ... in March one of our company representatives [Felix Hertzka] came to Manila to purchase surplus F-boats... [JavaChina's] only business here is the taking delivery of [these boats]. [After that is done] I intend to establish a fishing company here [or] marine repair and boat hire service."

Not only had Lucero no evidence whatever that Cheez was heading a Communist cell, but a lot of evidence that Cheez was just a day-dreamer who could not manage money, or keep a secret. Had he been a real Soviet agent, Cheez unquestionably would have been ordered shot by Stalin or Beria. But Lansdale knew he had a very gullible audience for his assertions.

Adding to their difficulties, Nina's tourist visa to The Philippines would soon run out. Cheez could fix the problem with a simple bribe, but he was too short of money. With a flash of insight, Nina became convinced that her trust in the Luceros, and everyone else, was misplaced. She remembered telling Mrs. Lucero that they knew lots of White Russians in Shanghai, assuming Mrs. Lucero would know White Russians were as anti-Bolshevik as you could be. Yet this was now being repeated to confirm that her husband was a secret agent.

Artificial pressure from Immigration officials was raised to unbearable levels after the interrogation by Detective Carlos. G-2 now knew from Cheez himself that he was broke, so there could be no better time to squeeze him. Nina and Georgie would be two victims of Project Manila.

Slightly more than a month after the Christmas Party, in February 1947, frantic last-minute efforts by Cheez failed, and they were turned down rudely by Philippine Immigration. Nina and Georgie were ordered to pack up and go back to Shanghai. Manila newspapers carried stories saying that they were among a group of Russians expelled "on suspicion of being Communists". To raise money for her trip and getting resettled in Shanghai, Cheez sold one of their remaining Jeeps and gave the cash to Nina. The sum would not have been enough to pay bribes to Immigration, but it would give her something to live on in Shanghai, sharing some with her father and invalid mother, who no longer received a subsistence allowance from JavaChina, in which they had once been investors. Memories were short.

Chapter 16 :

SITTING DUCKS

Once they heard from Detective Carlos that G-2 believed they were Soviet agents, Phil and Cheez should have left for Shanghai immediately, as Peterson had, taking Nina and Georgie with them. There they could find good jobs, or resume working for JavaChina. It should have been clear that most of their problems the past seven months were deliberate victimization by G-2. They might not know precisely who their enemies were, but if G-2 was behind it they were in grave danger. Not by being guilty, but by being not-guilty. In a place like The Philippines, arguing innocence would get them in deeper.

Although Phil was at times more practical, he could not believe this was serious. His American naivete was mixed with bull-headedness. His stubborn streak won out this time, telling friends and family: "I prefer to take my chances on some business venture with Cheez." He had money salted away in the bank for when he did go home, but not enough to satisfy him. No longer getting salaries or living expenses from JavaChina, they had convinced themselves they would start a new enterprise.

This overcame all sense of being in jeopardy.

Had it not been for being in very real danger, their money-making ideas made sense. In postwar Asia's battered cities, there was a strong market for timber, copra, and fish. If you were not in the supply end, there was money to be made hauling the raw materials to market, especially in an archipelago where remote islands and regions inaccessible by road needed boats to transport local products to Manila or Cebu.

Cheez's personal dream was to haul frozen fish from the out-islands to Manila, but this meant investing in facilities to freeze the fish, and equipping a boat with refrigeration to keep it frozen in transit. They briefly considered hauling copra to Manila from Baler on the east coast, then dropped it in favor of hauling hardwoods to Manila from the Bataan Peninsula, just across the bay. Forest industries had been robust in The Philippines before the war, when the ancient rainforest cover was reduced over 40 percent. By the end of 1946 that wood industry had not recovered, so there were critical shortages of wood for reconstruction, and rising prices. Two clever guys using modern equipment could make serious money. They discussed their ideas with friends to get useful feedback. But as so many of their friends were G-2 or police informants, this information reached enemies looking for ways to sabotage whatever venture they started. They were sitting ducks.

Most logging concessions belonged to rich landowners, or were inherited by upper middle-class professionals in Manila too busy to work them. Rural lumber mills were supplied by native loggers.

These local loggers used primitive techniques. They would use an axe to fell a single tree by hand, then hitch up two caribou to drag it out of the forest.

Using modern tools and bulldozers would give Phil and Cheez a big advantage. Once logs were hauled to a beach, they could be rafted together and towed to Manila by their LCM, the small landing craft that was part of their settlement from JavaChina. It was inadequate for bulk shipping, but was all they had and would do for towing floating logs.

They merely needed money to get the operation off the ground. At least, they might get a contract to tow logs, then expand to bigger logging operations.

Although he romanced a lot of pretty girls, taking them for a swim, a picnic, or for milkshakes at the Campus Drug Store, Phil saw a lot of Nena Nieto.

She was his pal, and had many useful contacts, among them men with inherited lumber concessions in out-of-the-way places including Bataan. She sounded them out. Nena had no reason to be suspicious when several of them got back to her straight away. Pretty rich girls never think twice about getting what they ask for.

One Sunday, Cheez, Nena, and Phil piled into a Jeep with several of Nena's wealthy friends, and drove over rough roads to Bataan where the men owned a lumber concession near the coastal town of Morong. Getting there was not easy:

"We followed the same route as the Bataan Death March, and boy it's even rough going in a Jeep. Took us six hours to go 100 miles."

They took no interest in Morong town, which they did not know was part of the Ilocano smuggling circuit feeding on goods stolen from Subic Bay Naval Base with the collusion of American officers and enlisted men. The circuit started at Manila, went north to Clark Air Base, then west to Subic Bay, south to Morong, and back east to Manila.

Goods looted from Clark or Subic moved south into the wilds of Bataan, piled up at Morong, then were trucked across Bataan to Manila.

The governor of Bataan province was part of the circuit, and had a holiday house in Morong, where he could keep an eye on his people and the movement of contraband. In 1946-1947, this circuit was run by the American Harry Stonehill, under the protection of the Quirino Machine.

"Our trip was to see where we could land our LCM on a beach, to load logs on board. We found many beautiful sloping beaches. The lumbermen offered us a contract paying 650 pesos per trip, hauling their logs. We figured we could make nearly one hundred percent profit since we could get fuel from friends on various ships without having to pay for it. Cheez and I were to sign a contract to make two trips per week." The ink was still wet on this contract when G-2 reported that Cheez had separately attempted to secure an extra loan for a P600,000 [$300,000] corporation to haul copra. "Unable to secure the money, he has lowered his sights and is now promoting a scheme to haul lumber into Manila from Bataan. He and Mehan estimate that they can gross P2,000 a month and made a trial run that earned them P650."

G-2 pricked up its ears at mention of logging in Bataan, because its rainforests and mountains were a stronghold of the "communist" Huks, which could be the real motive of these two Soviet agents.

Returning to Manila, Nena introduced them to a prosperous young doctor named Ricardo Q. Jimenez, who had been in medical school in America during the war. He had married into a rich family, had a clinic in a wealthy neighborhood full of doctors, and was raking money in delivering (or not delivering) the babies of wealthy young women. Jimenez also had a lumber concession near Morong, at Iman Point. A G-2 agent sent to check out Jimenez reported that the doctor was "About 30, 5'6", 150 lbs., well-built, brown complexion, thick wavy hair cut short. Drives a blue Jeep. Informants said Jimenez is very popular, related through his wife to the wealthy Mrs. Pelar Lerma, owner of a transportation company at 583 Antipolo St. Jimenez owns a hospital, with a good matron/midwife, so they make their living delivering babies, which are so plenty [sic] these days."

Dr. Jimenez told Phil and Cheez he could not operate his concession, because there was no way to get logs to market. He was willing to sell his logs to Phil and Cheez, if they would be in the area anyway, hauling logs for the other concessionaires. Jimenez said he could then gradually increase his production of logs. Visions of sugarplums were dancing before Cheez's eyes. If they only transported logs dragged to the beach by men working for all of these different concessionaires, there would be little overhead.

Dr. Jimenez saw the gleam in Cheez's eyes. The Russian was hooked: If Chirskoff were an Eskimo, he'd sell himself a refrigerator. Jimenez realized he did not need to put money into the venture. These two dreamers would do everything themselves.

"Suddenly Dr. Jimenez informed us his money had run out. The Doctor was now, in effect, out of the logging business. So we offered to take control of the concession from soup to nuts for half of all profit in the lumber operation. Jimenez accepted. It was irresistible on the face of it. Without investing a cent of our own money, we now owned half of a valuable lumber concession. But if the concession was going to run profitably, we needed our own equipment. We started inquiring all over Manila ." Everyone wanted in on it.

G-2 reported: "Chirskoff has visited the office of Material Distributors Co., and purchased for his lumber business two truck-tractors and two truck-trailers, plus a crane, all financed by a very low down-payment (only P6,000) and a large unpaid balance in 90 days."

The owner of Manila Distributors claimed he had heard Cheez owned a Cadillac and was in the market for heavy equipment. The Cadillac had now been sold, but the only other one in the islands was easily located by Cheez. Manila Distributors took it as down payment on the two trailers and a D7 Caterpillar tractor.

Meantime, Phil sold JavaChina's two remaining PT-boats for 12,000 pesos, to pay the balance on the D7. Cats were slow but rugged and powerful, moving on tank treads that provided excellent traction on hills.

"We now owned the D7 outright so we mortgaged it, and used the proceeds to buy some more equipment. We bought two more Cats, a D4 and a D6, one more trailer, and a large generator. With such a remote lumber camp, the generator was a real necessity. Cheez and I had every cent tied up in our equipment, and had bought over P21,000 worth of other equipment on a 90-day plan."

The unwary Phil and Cheez were now going to move all the valuable equipment they had purchased on credit right into a town that specialized in stealing heavy equipment for logging, cannibalizing trucks to disguise their origins, then selling them on to other concessionaires at bargain prices. Unaware of the hidden dangers of doing business in or near Morong, Phil got to work loading twelve 55-gallon drums of diesel fuel in the stern of the LCM. Manila Distributors sent a heavy vehicle operator called a Cat Skinner to back the D7 and D6 Caterpillars onto the LCM. Manila Distributors also promised to send another Cat Skinner to Iman Point the next morning to drive the Cats off the LCM and take them a mile or so to Moron for safe keeping.

Phil and a young Filipino assistant named Tim left Manila aboard the LCM the following morning, and drove the LCM up on the chosen beach at Iman Point. Surf was heavy, so the Cats had to be taken off quickly before the Landing Craft's bilge pump choked up with swirling sand.

Manila Distributor's Cat Skinner was not there.

Phil said: "I knew nothing about operating Cats, and Tim less than I. The D7 alone weighed over 32,000 pounds. It was impossible to back the LCM off the beach until the tractors were unloaded. The boat was taking a terrific beating from the surf so I couldn't afford to wait for Manila Distributors to show. I had to figure out how to start and drive the Cats off the LCM myself."

Both Cats had diesel engines started by two-cylinder gasoline 'pony' engines. The big Cat in the bow of the LCM had a pony engine with a crank on top. After switching on what he thought would be the ignition, Phil cranked and cranked. Nothing happened.

He gave up on the D7 and turned his attention to the smaller D6 in the middle of the LCM. Rather than a crank on top of its pony engine, it had a pulley similar to those on outboard motors. He wrapped the starter rope around the pulley and -- expecting to be disappointed -- yanked as hard as he could.

The D6 pony motor started instantly, causing havoc. "The tracks began moving the D6 backward."

Both Cats had been loaded after the drums of diesel-fuel. So the D6 had been backed up snug against the drums to make room for the D7 in the front of the boat. The trip to Bataan had been a relatively short journey in calm seas, so there had seemed to be no need to lash anything down. When Phil had driven the landing craft hard up on the beach to assure a solid position for unloading the tractors, the massive bulk of the Cats had moved them forward slightly.

With only the stern of the LCM in the water, at a steep angle, the tractors were tilted backwards.

The Skinner in Manila had left the Cats in reverse gear, so engine compression would keep their treads from moving, but Phil had pushed and pulled every lever until he guessed the gears were in neutral.

Instead, they were in low-reverse.

On such an incline, the pony engine had just enough power for the Cat to crawl back toward the LCM's pilothouse, climbing up over the 50-gallon drums, crushing them and spewing diesel oil everywhere.

Each time a drum burst, the Cat climbed the next and crushed it, creeping inexorably toward the stern.

Searching frantically for the off-switch, Phil realized that after the oil drums would come the destruction of the pilothouse and all its controls, after which the Cat would climb over the stern and sink in the surf.

He knew small pony engines ran on a magneto, with a steel spring to stop the engine. The kill-spring had to be held down several seconds. But with diesel oil everywhere, Phil could not stand up, and his finger kept slipping off the spring.

"I ended up on my knees crawling along the moving track like a treadmill, trying to stay in place long enough to kill the engine, while my knees took a terrific beating from the metal cleats.

"After nearly losing some fingers, I finally stopped the starter engine and the Cat came to a halt inches from the pilothouse. Before trying to start the D6 again, I'd make darn sure the transmission was in neutral."

When his panic subsided and he thought he had things figured out, with the Cat definitely in neutral, he restarted the pony engine, and let it start the big D6 diesel engine. When he opened the throttle, the mighty machine sprang to life, smoke pouring out its exhaust.

The D7 had been loaded aboard last so he used the D6 to push the D7 onto the beach. Sweating with relief, he got back on the landing craft and backed it off the beach to anchor it safely outside the surf line. With Tim watching at a wary distance, Phil practiced driving the D6, starting, stopping, turning, until he thought he could drive it to Morong. The D7 still would not start, so he had Tim sit at its controls to work the clutch, while Phil pushed with the D6. By late in the day, they finally got the D7 started. After revving it up till it ran smooth, he left Tim to guard the smaller Cat and the LCM, and headed for Morong on the D7.

Cats did not have steering wheels like cars or trucks. They had two levers called frictions that controlled each steel tread, and two brake pedals, one for each tread. To turn left or right, you slowed one tread while speeding up the other, like an Army tank. Depending on how well you did this, the Cat either turned slowly, or spun on its own footprint. On the way to Morong, Phil began to relax, using the friction levers as if they were hand-breaks, when in fact they were clutches that released each tread. That became clear when he started down a hill in high gear, with the throttle wide open. Coming to a hairpin curve, he pulled on the left lever expecting the Cat to turn left.

"Boy, was I in for a surprise!"

The Cat lurched to the right, and all 16 tons of Cat and 180 pounds of Phil careened down the embankment, peeling off the shoulder of the road. By some miracle, the Cat did not roll over. Getting it back up on the road proved impossible for a novice, so Phil took a deep breath and drove on down the slope to the road below the hairpin, and continued to cut corners that way to Morong.

They had permission from the mayor of Morong for both Cats to be parked next to the Town Hall a few days. Local residents had never seen such big yellow-painted machines. The entire population turned out. Worried about Tim and the D6, he hitched a ride back to the beach, where Tim was greatly relieved to see him. If roving bandits had emerged from the rainforest while Phil was gone, the LCM and D6 would have been looted and Tim probably killed. After driving the D6 to Morong to park beside the D7, he was taken back to the cove again as the sun set on the South China Sea.

Swimming back out to the oily LCM, they pulled away from the beach as daylight vanished. Dead tired, they rounded the tip of Bataan by Corrigedor Island, and saw Manila as a haze of light on the eastern horizon.

The logging operation had got off on the wrong foot, but things could be worse.

While Tim and Phil cleaned up the LCM, Cheez got the logging operation up and running, only to have more difficulties. Local teams of loggers hired from Morong were painfully slow, their work habits infuriating. A team would work a few days, then disappear without notice to hunt wild boar, till rice fields, or gather rattan. When they returned to work, and discovered other men doing their jobs, they threatened to kill them.

Getting logs to Manila also proved far more difficult than expected. Harnessed with chains to the bulldozers, the ends of each heavy towed log plowed into the soft forest floor.

After two months working the Jimenez concession, there were not enough logs at the beach to tow to Manila. Not a single board foot had been sold, not a peso raised. House rent was past due, wages had to be paid, and the 90-day loan on equipment was fast coming due.

Manila Police and G-2 were kept informed by Dr. Jimenez and Captain Lucero. It seems odd that a small-time enterprise should attract so much attention. But the dossier shows monitoring as intense as if a secret germ warfare facility had been located. Lucero reported: "No lumber has been produced and funds are low. Their LCM has proven to be inadequate for hauling logs. ...they have employed some 15 Filipinos. ... The venture is ... handicapped by a lack of proper tools and equipment. ...two bulldozers and a few hand tools seem to be all they have."

Phil was eyeballed by agents hanging around the fast-food Metro Grill. Every week Cheez popped into the Lucero's house for a meal and regaled them with anecdotes.

He even offered to serve as a spy for G-2. Pointing to a man in the Metro Grill who was a Russian, he told Lucero: "You see I could be a big help to you boys if you keep me around."

With Nina and Georgie gone, the house on Roberts Road was a white elephant. Phil dismissed the two young maids, and the nanny Esperanza, then paid past due rent and moved the furniture to a friend's house for storage. Things were not going well. Phil:

"I was concerned about leaving Cheez running the lumber concession by himself. We had hoped to have 210 logs ready to ship by the end of April. This would have brought in around 7,000 pesos. Unfortunately, the middle of May found us still with no logs ready to ship. And at that point Cheez got sick."

Sleeping in the rainforest in an Army surplus jungle-hammock was uncomfortable and unhealthy, even with a rain hood and mosquito net. On a diet of rice and tinned corned-beef, Cheez had got an infected tooth, nearly died from high fever, and had to be hospitalized in Manila.

Phil heard of a crew of professional loggers from the Visayan Islands now available in Manila. He hired the Visayans, loaded them and their gear on to rented trucks, and headed for Iman Point while Cheez remained in the hospital. When they reached the camp, he fired all the men from Morong.

These Visayan woodsmen were renowned as fearless. Larger in stature than the Filipinos in Morong, each was armed with a razor-sharp bolo, and relished a challenge.

Local troublemakers might feel tough, but they were riff-raff, afraid to confront the Visayans. Instead, they vandalized the camp when everyone was out working, stealing anything lying around. Each evening the Cats had to be driven back to camp.

During the day, armed guards went into the forest with the tractors and crews, and a day-guard was posted at the camp with a rifle. This ended most of the harassment, but pot-shots were still being fired at the Visayans.

A college-educated forest guard employed by the government appeared as if by chance, and marked the most profitable species that had reached maturity, by-passing younger trees to insure future viability of the forest.

The Visayans felled the trees and limbed them on the spot, sizing them to lengths suitable for mills. Phil bulldozed several roadside clearings where they assembled logs. Men called Hookers walked beside the Cats choosing logs ready to drag. These logs were so heavy they had to be hooked-up correctly so they did not plow into the turf. One end of a choker cable was fastened to a log, the other to a Cat. The Hookers chose the smaller end so each log lifted slightly as it was pulled, skidding along behind the Cat, rather than digging-in. It was dangerous work. Phil almost rolled the big D7 over on himself while backing down a steep incline. To load the trucks they stretched cables between tall trees, rigged pulleys midway, and threaded loading cables through the pulleys. When enough logs were at the landing areas, one end of each log was hoisted by the small D4 Cat hauling on the pulley, as a truck backed under the log.

If logs were too heavy for the D4, the D6 was brought down.

Once fully loaded, the trucks carried the logs to Iman Point, where they were rolled off down a slope to the beach. Some got hung up halfway, so Phil found a gentler slope where he bulldozed a road straight to the beach. Under so much strain, the trucks frequently needed new clutches and axles.

The next step was to get the logs to Manila. When they tried rafting logs together and towing them to Manila, the fresh-cut hardwoods were too dense to float, and wallowed in the surf. Phil lashed empty oil drums to them as floats, but on the way to Manila several logs broke free of the awkward raft and floated away like giant rolls of silver dollars. Even with a capacity of 30-tons, the LCM had to strain to move the log rafts.

Seeing their plight, the Chinese mill operators in Manila took advantage, offering a lower price than previously agreed. The new price was so low Phil decided they were better off selling their logs at Iman Point, and letting the Chinese mill operators pick up the logs with a bigger 150-ton capacity LCT (Landing Craft Tank).

"The LCT could carry about 60 or 70 logs the size we cut. We paid 5 centavos per board foot for the haulage, so it cost us 3,000 pesos a week to have the Chinese transport the logs to Manila, but we did not have to haul them ourselves. We also had to pay 1,210 pesos a week for the trucks we rented. Until I cut the overhead, our profit margin was small.

Now we had fewer men, but they were the Visayan professionals, so production increased enormously. We were working ten hours a day, seven days a week."

They still had to pay the 90-day loan. Anxiety and misery aside, the camp on the rain forested promontory overlooked the China Sea, and the cove below was beautiful. After a day in the forest, everyone returned to camp caked in sweat, ready for a swim. Phil had no time to shave, and grew a beard.

"One night while sleeping soundly in my jungle-hammock, I was startled awake when something landed on my stomach. I was nose to nose with a 5-foot monitor lizard. I got a few scratches but the Visayans cooked the lizard for dinner."

As work became more efficient, they were shipping about 60,000 board feet per week, enough for two LCT boatloads. Thanks to his stubbornness, and the professionalism of the Visayans, Phil had been remarkably successful in putting things right. That being the case, it was time again for Lansdale's G-2 to trip them up.

"After roughing it over a month, I no longer was as enthusiastic about logging as I used to be. Ever since Cheez and I started, there had been friction with the locals. Our machinery was too massive for a caribou to drag away, so these simple-minded people tried to destroy our tractors, to put us out of business."

Phil thought at first that it was only pilfering by simple-minded villagers. Then it dawned on him that there was nothing random about it.

Systematic troublemaking was going on.

"While Cheez was still hospitalized, I decided to upgrade our trucks, so we could stop paying outlandish rental for the beat-up trucks we were using. I left my trusted Visayans in charge and went to Manila, where I approached a friend, Jerry Widrin, who agreed to purchase several Deuce-and-a-Half trucks in good condition and rent them to Cheez and me, with an option to buy.

Jerry Widrin had been Phil's first friend in Manila the previous year. He had just arrived in Manila from California as a U.S. Army PFC when atom bombs were dropped on Hiroshima and Nagasaki, ending the war and making an invasion of the Japanese Home Islands unnecessary.

Widrin decided to stay in the Philippines and go into business buying and selling surplus equipment and ship cargoes, which it made no sense to haul back to America. He set up Phil-American Trading Company in Manila, making a lot of money. Only 21, Widrin was a good looking square-faced guy with curly hair, much savvier than Phil, Cheez, or Pete, about the way things really worked. He took pains to avoid getting involved with the really bad guys. He had been on the periphery of some of Harry Stonehill's business deals for surplus equipment, sometimes gambled at Stonehill's casinos, but refused to be drawn in. So he knew quite a lot about the Quirino Machine, the black market, and the underworld. He was a good man to know, able to get things done.

Smart. Long antennae.

After four days in Manila, as Phil was preparing to return to Iman Point, a Visayan appeared. He said several men had come into the cove at twilight on a banca dugout with an outboard motor, and opened fire with machine-guns and rifles.

"The fact that they had a shiny new outboard motor showed they were not casual vandals. These guys had money and a mission. Our Visayans, who had only old Enfield rifles, fled for their lives. I could only imagine what would become of the camp and our equipment if I didn't get there right away. With Cheez still in the hospital, Jerry offered to go with me. So did my assistant Tim. I loaded the Jeep with supplies for any contingency. Food stores had been raided so we bought groceries, and spare parts including fan-belts, lights, ignition wires, carburetors and other parts that had been stolen from us repeatedly. Jerry and I both carried licensed automatics but did not want to be outgunned. One of his friends in the U.S. Army Military Police loaned us a Thompson submachine-gun, and a Garand rifle, plus ammunition for both, and we headed off to Iman Point.

"When we reached Iman Point, I was not prepared for what I saw. My men had fled, and our camp had been burned to the ground by the raiders.

"The diesel engine of our big D7 Cat had been removed, leaving only the frame. The small D4 tractor had been burned, along with our shacks. But my Visayans bringing the D6 back to camp had heard the shooting and managed to drive the Cat away as they fled to Morong, saving it.

"Luckily, I had already returned the rented trucks to their owner in Manila. Other than that, about the only good news was we found no dead bodies.

"Soon as Jerry and I realized the camp had been vandalized and looted, we set out with Tim to find the men responsible. Jerry and I had now been in The Philippines about two years, and had seen this sort of thing happen again and again, without the culprits ever being caught by the police. Either the police were lazy, or in cahoots.

Examining the scene, we found a perfect set of truck tire marks, made when they backed a truck up to hoist the diesel engine aboard and haul it away. Luckily, the US Army only produced tires with two types of tread, one a chevron V-tread, and a more common diagonal tread. Here, three of the truck's four rear tires were diagonal tread, and the fourth one had chevron Vs. This gave us a fingerprint of the suspect truck, and a good chance of finding it. We went first to Morong, the most obvious place to start, saw only one truck, which we immediately identified by its tires. Also, the cargo bed was wet with lubricating oil, and was dented in a way that only could have been made by something as heavy as our missing big diesel engine. All Cats and their engines were factory-painted school-bus yellow, and yellow paint marks were all over the truck bed. The truck's owner lived in a nipa hut beside the truck. We confronted him and took him to the local jail inside the town hall. The only officer on duty was not interested in cooperating but after some argument he reluctantly placed the truck owner under arrest."

Facing 15 years in prison on charges of attempted murder, armed-robbery, theft, and vandalism, the man quickly confessed. He said he and his brother jointly owned the truck, while employing a teenage driver. The night of the raid they were approached by six men, three of whom had come to Morong only recently. Those men asked to borrow the truck and driver.

"Jerry and I tracked down the brother and the young driver, and hauled them to jail also. The young driver's testimony corroborated everything. He also identified the six raiders by name.

"We set out to find them, and to see if we could find any more of our stolen equipment. We started with the largest house in town, a well-built wood frame structure with a thatch roof. Hanging under its open carport we found a new outboard motor of the same type used in the raid. These were uncommon in remote villages like Morong.

"We found no one on the property, but a curious young Filipino boy had taken to following us around. He said it was the Governor's house and outboard motor. It had to be his rural retreat, since the Governor's official mansion was in the provincial capital, Baclaren.

"The boy then led us behind the old church where he pointed out the yellow engine block from our D7.

"Searching the immediate area, we found a cache of small engine parts inside the church, and the radiator and other tractor parts hidden in a nearby dry well.

"By this time, Morong's Chief of Police appeared. He had heard about Jerry and me nosing around, and insisted we have a police escort, obviously to keep tabs on us. From then on, policemen with burp guns accompanied us everywhere, and the little boy wisely disappeared. We resumed our hut-to-hut search for the raiders. In several huts, I saw dishes and eating utensils from our camp. I kept pointing this out to Jerry, but he signaled me to be quiet. I wanted to confront the occupants of the huts, but Jerry was worried, and didn't want me to provoke more trouble than we already had.

"We didn't find the raiders, so we headed back to the jail, where there was a big surprise for us. The two truck owners and their driver were gone, and in their cell were three of the meanest looking thugs I had ever seen. These turned out to be three of the six raiders, and apparently had walked in out-of-the blue to surrender. The other three raiders had vanished, probably going back to the provincial capital of Baclaren. It was not much of a stretch to imagine they had been sent to Morong by the Governor, given the use of his new outboard motor to carry out their raid.

"These three guys looked like professional gangsters, rough men covered with scars. They sure weren't timid Filipinos. When I questioned them, they made obscene gestures, cursed, and spat at me.

"Jerry had made an impressive list of charges, so we went to the Police Chief's office to lodge a formal complaint.

"I was puzzled when the Chief seemed completely indifferent, but soon discovered the reason.

"As we left the Chief's office, I saw a seat from one of our Cats tucked behind his open door. When I pointed the seat out to Jerry, I saw dread cross his face. With his intuition confirmed that everyone in Morong was in on the raid, Jerry was seriously scared. In a den of thieves, he knew we could easily be murdered.

"All the pieces were falling into place. In our search of the village, we had uncovered our own stolen equipment plus a rich cache of other expensive goods we assumed were also stolen. Judging by items we saw, we had stumbled on a smuggling ring that somehow had free access to whatever they wanted to steal from the U.S. Naval Base at Subic Bay. Presumably, all six raiders were part of the Quirino Machine, with family ties to everyone in Morong, including the Mayor and Chief of Police.

Having found the new outboard motor in the Governor's carport, even he was implicated.

"Realizing how dangerous this was becoming, we sent Tim to the city of Olongapo near Subic Bay, to summon the U.S. Military Police. The next day, Tim returned instead with a Circuit Judge with the name of Ochoa. I was disappointed, since Ochoa might be part of the mafia, but he turned out to be just the opposite. Overruling all objections from Morong officials, Judge Ochoa arraigned the prisoners, set a trial date for later in the week, and said he would be back for the trial.

"Later in the day, Widrin and I returned to the jail to find the cell doors open and the three thugs gone.

"The Chief and his jailer were nowhere in sight. When we rushed to the Mayor's office to sound the alarm, the Mayor shrugged and explained that everyone had gone home for lunch. I was astounded. These were dangerous men facing prison for attempted murder. Why would they return on their own? But the Mayor proved to be right. They did return to jail after lunch, apparently obeying orders from somebody.

"As promised, Circuit Judge Ochoa returned to town several days later and presided over a hearing. He was surprisingly fair and straightforward. Though we had no witnesses, the circumstantial evidence was obviously very strong because we had found all that was stolen. Judge Ochoa made the thugs agree to pay us restitution in the amount of 24,600 pesos, if we dropped all charges."

It sounded too good to be true. Phil thought everything was going to be okay because the judge had the sense to propose restitution rather than prison. Surely the thugs would see the logic and do the right thing. They did, but what they thought was the right thing. Shortly after the trial, Judge Ochoa was found murdered. The death certificate said he died of 'heart failure'.

"This woke me up.

"I decided that rebuilding our operation at Morong wasn't worth the expense or the risk. I once viewed The Philippines as a land of opportunity. When Cheez and I left JavaChina, we had so many business opportunities in mind it was hard to choose between them.

"In retrospect, due to the Filipino system, it was all fool's gold.

"I returned to Manila and told Cheez what happened in Morong and that I was quitting the logging business. Cheez disagreed, saying he was sure we could still make a go of it, with the equipment we recovered and the better trucks. But my bad experience in Morong, and the obvious fact that most of the people in Morong were targeting us, had made up my mind. I wanted to liquidate all of our assets. Cheez begged me to sign my interest over to him, so he could keep logging. We had a long discussion."

Cheez still dreamed of becoming established in The Philippines. He argued that in spite of the raid, their assets were still substantial. They held exclusive rights to harvest trees from the concession. Eventually that could be worth millions of pesos, once the trees could be cut efficiently and delivered to the mill. They still had equity in the Cats. There was a good cache of logs remaining at the roadside clearings, which could be sold for quick cash. Finally, there was the 24,600 pesos compensation owed by the Morong thugs, assuming they did not vanish.

"My response to Cheez was that listing assets, and laying your hands on the assets were different matters. I didn't relish the idea of trying to recover our equipment from Morong, or collecting the money from the cutthroats. Two of the Cats needed major repairs. Finally, it seemed pretty unlikely the Visayans would return, so a new crew of loggers would have to be hired.

"Personally, I doubted that Cheez could get the business running again, but I had to admire his grit and determination. In the end, I agreed with the proviso that I got the LCM in exchange for Jerry's trucks. My new plan was to get out of The Philippines, in a way that required a boat. Since the LCM was no good to Cheez, but he needed the trucks for logging, we were both happy." Their partnership was now over.

Cheez's visa had now expired, so he was in the country illegally, with nowhere else to go.

He was no longer welcome in Shanghai or Manila because G-2 was spreading the word, falsely portraying him as a Soviet agent involved with the Huks.

"As far as I knew, he was not a communist, or anything like one, but he had been smeared."

Cheez had been "born in interesting times".

Chapter 17 :

ENTRAPMENT

When Cheez would not 'listen to reason', Phil began hanging out with Jerry Widrin instead. At first Cheez was disappointed, then offended, then deeply annoyed. Phil had ditched him and washed his hands of their joint-venture; in disgust, he left Manila for Bataan to reassemble their logging equipment, and to get the operation running again, either there or somewhere else. What else could he do, if he wanted to bring Nina and Georgie back from Shanghai. He was profoundly saddened that all their money and hopes had been pinned on this venture, only to have Phil change his mind and abandon their joint effort.

G-2 noted this ill-will with glee: "Chirskoff and Mehan appear to be on bad terms. Mehan ... sold a number of Chirskoff's personal belongings." Doing so without asking Cheez first crossed an invisible line.

Phil and Jerry Widrin now planned to make one last grab at the brass ring before both left The Philippines for good. No more dealing with cagey U.S. Army officers; no more haggling with JavaChina; no more saboteurs or informers; no more brushing elbows with the likes of Harry Stonehill. They'd just load up the remaining LCM with cargo to sell in British North Borneo, then get out of The Philippines and back to the States. With North Borneo prices far higher than those in Manila, their profits would pay for the trip home, and a new start.

Originally, it had been Widrin's plan. North Borneo's towns and cities including Sandakan had been flattened by Allied bombing of Japanese installations in 1945. Now the British Protectorate was trying to rebuild, hungry for anything and everything. Jerry had made the trip once before, getting an LCM crammed full of cargo from Manila to North Borneo, where the cargo brought high prices, and the LCM was sold for a fat profit. Jerry could not make the trip alone because he was not a mariner. The previous trip had been done with a partner who was a skilled skipper and navigator. This time Phil would be the skipper, Jerry the first mate.

Although purchased for JavaChina, the LCM was part of the exchange made by Winkelman to square accounts with Cheez and Phil, and was registered in Phil's name, but shared with Cheez. In exchange for the two Army trucks Widrin had bought as hire-purchase for the logging operation, Cheez relinquished his share in the LCM. To protect it from being seized by creditors or other 'dark forces', Phil had the LCM re-registered in Widrin's name alone.

Despite all the trouble in Morong, Jerry and Phil were in no hurry. They intended to spend several weeks getting the LCM spruced up, painted and prepared for the island-hopping voyage south, while taking their time choosing the most profitable cargo to put aboard.

Because space was tight in the harbor, the LCM was moored in the mouth of the Pasig River, rafted up to other boats near the seawall. Theirs was the fourth boat out. To save money, and make sure nothing happened to boat or cargo, the two men slept aboard.

On the night of July 15, 1947, Jerry remained aboard while Phil spent a long evening with Nena Nieto, not returning to the LCM till early the following morning, just before dawn.

As Phil started down the seawall toward the rafted LCM, he was alarmed to see a Filipino cop lurking in the gloom. Instead of going straight across the rafted boats to the LCM, Phil made an unannounced social call on the Irishman tied up alongside. Paddy hushed Phil up, took him below, and gave a quick reprise of the night's events:

"Widrin was trying to start the generator when the Flip police swarmed onto your boat like commandos. There were so many, I thought my own boat would sink!" He said Jerry was dragged away in handcuffs. Paddy was not sure why. But in their search of the vessel, the police had uncovered the weapons lent to them by Widrin's friend in the Military Police, for protection against the raiders at Iman Point: the Thompson submachine-gun, its long clip of .45 ammunition, the Garand rifle with ammunition, and an old Japanese rifle. Possessing guns and ammunition was common in The Philippines, hardly a crime. But the police claimed that Phil and Jerry were planning to smuggle guns to Borneo.

It was not Widrin they were after. Widrin was being staked out like a goat to entrap Phil with gun-running charges. Not thinking things through, Phil acted too fast. He went straight to the police station where Widrin said he would be released once a 5,000 peso bail was paid. It was unclear whether the gun-running allegation would be dropped.

All Phil's cash was tied up in the LCM and acquisition of cargo. For Widrin's bail, he turned to plywood-maker Max Zalevsky, the same man who had falsely told G-2 that Cheez had "communist tendencies".

But Zalevsky was well connected, and he had the bankroll to guarantee Widrin's bond with the local gendarmes.

Zalevsky did post Widrin's bail, without telling Phil. So Phil raised a similar amount and returned to Police Headquarters to liberate his friend. Jerry was already gone, but Phil was taken forcibly to Detective Sergeant Salas, who proceeded to arrest him, not for gun-running, but for fraud.

"I didn't know what Estafa meant, but Salas read the charges to me."

Estafa was shorthand for Commonwealth Act No. 303: "Every employer, including the head of every government office ... shall pay the salaries and wages of his employees and laborers at least once every two weeks... Failure of the employer to pay his employees or laborers ... shall prima facie be considered a fraud."

MadDog Mabini had encouraged Captain Dimuahuan, Captain Vilamor, and certain members of their crews, to charge of non-payment of wages, claiming that JavaChina had swindled the crews they hired. Mabini knew he had received half the wages in advance from Phil, covering all pay up to actual departure for China, which never came to pass. Because of their bizarre behavior, those captains and crews had been fired without earning the second half of the wages. But Mabini refused to accept.

Although Cheez and Phil were only employees of JavaChina, the lawsuit cited them as company officers. Winkelman had told Phil that JavaChina alone would be responsible for the lawsuit if it went to court, but Winkelman was out of reach in Shanghai.

Estafa lawsuits were one of the most lucrative rackets in the Philippine justice system. Cases dragged on for decades. Many were dismissed because of "malicious prosecution ... initiated deliberately by the defendant knowing that his charges were false and groundless."

G-2 knew all about Phil's savings account in a California bank, where his wages had been deposited regularly by the Army Transport

Corps. This information was passed on to Filipino detectives, so the whole Estafa case was a shakedown to hassle Phil and Cheez. Phil was fuming, because Bail was fixed at 10,000 pesos.

"I offered to write a check, but Salas first demanded my treasured pearl-handled Colt .45 automatic, which I was licensed to carry. I refused. Salas stepped back as one of his officers fingerprinted me, then demanded my Colt again. I said, only if I got a receipt. I didn't want to give up my .45, but I was stalling for time, to size things up. Salas ordered a clerk at a desk by the door to cobble up a receipt on a soiled piece of department letterhead. While he did, I fiddled around at the clerk's desk, until Salas was distracted by another cop. Thanking the clerk for the receipt, I asked him to tell Salas I would stop by in the morning to recover my pistol. Then I simply strolled out of the room.

"I hurried to the front door of police headquarters only to bump into two detectives coming in. One reached out as if to stop me. I dodged him, walking fast and calling out: 'Can't talk now! Got a hot date. Have to run.'"

Phil did not wait to see if they were convinced. He jumped on his Harley, kick-started, and sped away.

G-2 recorded the whole affair in detail:

"On 15 July, 1947, detectives of the Manila Secret Service (formerly MPD) raided the LCM anchored in the Pasig River between Jones and Santa Cruz bridges. This boat was purchased in 1946 from the Foreign Liquidation Commission by the JavaChina Trading Co. through its Manila Agent, V.N. Chirskoff, and was registered in the name of Philip A. Mehan, an American merchant mariner in the employ of Chirskoff and JavaChina. Prior to the raid, Mehan had stated his intention of taking the boat to Borneo for sale at a higher price than offered in Manila and had arranged with American ex-G.I. Gerald M. Widrin to purchase Chirskoff's interest in the boat by the transfer of two six-by-six trucks.

Because of the many debts owed by Mehan & Chirskoff, the papers on the boat were transferred to the name of Widrin, thus effectively stopping any possible attachment proceedings on the part of creditors. The raiders, acting on a tip that Widrin and Mehan intended to smuggle firearms and ammunition to Borneo, arrested Widrin and confiscated the weapons found on board... Widrin was questioned at length and at first agreed to make a statement, but after signing it, changed his mind, wrestled it away from the detectives and tore it up. While in custody, Widrin contacted two Russians held for deportation since the middle of 1945... On the 16th [of July], bail in the amount of P5,000 was posted by Widrin through a bonding company at a fee of $400, after Zalevsky had signed as co-guarantor..., and he was released from custody. On the 17th of July, Widrin was able to have all charges against him dismissed, although the weapons and ammunition were confiscated.

Meanwhile, Mehan had been arrested and escaped.

When Phil ducked out of police headquarters under the very nose of Detective Salas, he headed for Nena Nieto's house, a villa owned by her father in one of Manila's luxurious gated communities. She had told Phil it was considered off-limits to police. Hiding his motorcycle in back, Phil spent that night sleeping uneasily on Nena's couch, uncertain what would happen next. Officially, he was now a fugitive.

The truth was further garbled by journalists. The day after Phil slipped out of the detective bureau, the MANILA NEWS ran this:

POLICE REARREST ALLEGED RUNNER

Several hours after questioning and releasing Philip Mehan, 21, local merchant and ex-GI, Manila police late last night again mobilized to effect his arrest on the strength of a warrant issued by Judge Filipe Natividad of the Manila Court of First Instance, charging him with illegal trafficking in firearms and ammunition. Police sources were secretive as to the exact nature of the charges against Mehan. It was indicated, however, that it has something to do with connecting him to the alleged smuggling of arms from the Islands to points in British North Borneo. Judge Natividad was understood to have fixed bail for his temporary release at P10,000. Earlier yesterday, Mehan appeared at headquarters to deny having given or sold firearms to Gerald M. Widrin, 21, another ex-GI, in whose barge the police seized a cache of firearms and ammunition Tuesday night during a raid. ... A pistol in the possession of Mehan was found to be duly licensed. ... he was subsequently released. Meanwhile, a complaint for illegal possession of firearms was preferred against Widren by the police yesterday. The city Fiscal

was understood to have recommended a bail of P5,000 for [Widrin's] temporary release.

In fact, neither Phil nor Jerry was formally charged then or at any other time with gunrunning, or any other charges connected to the borrowed guns. Jerry was jailed overnight, then released on bail without charges. In print, to cover up his letting a prisoner walk out of police headquarters, Sergeant Salas insisted he had released Phil.

Other newspapers ran similar stories.

Nena brought Phil copies of all the newspapers. Phil now had a wild plan. In the morning he would try to get to Ft. McKinley, the U.S. Army Base on the other side of the Pasig River. There, technically on American soil, he would be out of the reach of Philippine legal enforcers. He had a friend there who might help.

Hopping into a taxi early the next day, wearing his old Army Transport Corps uniform, Phil saw a Manila Police Jeep tail. He told his cabbie that the Jeep's occupants were armed thugs out to kill him.

Just as they approached the bridge over the Pasig River, the driver panicked and tried to get ahead of other cars by swerving into the oncoming lane, dodging several head-on collisions. The police Jeep was left far behind, snarled in honking traffic. Dropping Phil at the gate to the Army base, the cabbie roared away, forgetting to collect his fare.

Safe on base, and less conspicuous in his uniform, Phil took refuge in a friend's office, making urgent phone calls. The first thing he learned from a girlfriend was that Detective Salas had sent men to the homes of every girl Phil had dated -- and some he barely knew -- telling them he had been bragging about sleeping with her. Phil was dismayed. He would have to do a lot of fence-mending.

He was now a fugitive, in a foreign country. The Philippine government, the underworld, and U.S. Army G-2 were all hunting for him. Self preservation would have suggested escaping from the country as quickly as possible. In the past he never hesitated to leave The Philippines illegally, without an exit permit, whenever it was unavoidable. Now, when he was in serious trouble, he felt he had to stay to clear himself. He refused to leave until he had both justice and vindication, in a place famous for its absence. If he fled the country, the fraud charges might follow him to China, even back to America.

He failed to see that this time, if he was caught, he would go directly to Bilibad Prison. There he would be unable to defend himself against whatever charges were trumped-up, and might be found dead one morning. Bilibad was a notorious and vile place, its name a corruption of an old Pidgen term for criminals: "Billy-Bad".

While holed up at Fort McKinley in this state of mind, bent on justice, he made phone contact with a lawyer named Teodoro, a former judge and prominent Manila attorney. Phil expected Teodoro to force the Philippine legal system to recognize his innocence, something thousands of Filipinos had tried to do, unsuccessfully. Had Phil known this, he might have tried a different plan.

Slipping out of Ft. McKinley to meet privately with Teodoro, he patiently explained the history of his dispute with the Seamen's Union. Familiar with Estafa scams, Teodoro assured Phil there was no reason to worry, for he would represent Phil before the courts.

"You mean this has to go to court? I'm guilty till proven innocent?"

"You just revealed your innocence, but could still be found guilty."

Phil told Teodoro about his run-ins with Nena Nieto's father, the thugs in Morong who destroyed the lumber concession, the murder of Judge Ochua, and the bizarre Christmas allegation from Sergeant Detective Carlos that he and Cheez were suspected of being communist agents helping the Huks. It might have been wiser not to tell Teodoro so much, because the attorney now grasped that Phil was in the grip of a giant squid. Being Phil's defender could be dangerous. Teodoro told Phil the first thing he had to do was 'regularize' his situation with the police and the court house. This meant turning himself in, asking to get out on bail. Phil heard this with a spasm of dread. He had bamboozled the detectives twice in the last twenty-four hours, waltzing out of headquarters, then the car chase to Ft. McKinley. They would not take all this kindly. Teodoro assured Phil it was a simple matter of negotiating terms of surrender, paying bail, after which he would not be in custody, pending trial.

All Phil needed, he said, was a guarantee from someone influential. Only one man could help him. Back in the golden days at the Manila Hotel, he had become friendly with Dr. Victor Buencamino, the head of the School of Veterinary Science and onetime advisor to President

Quezon, a rich man to boot. His family were among Pampanga's biggest landowners, with thousands of acres of sugar cane. When they had met, the doctor told Phil if he ever needed help to call him.

At that moment, Buencamino was at a reception in the Manila Hotel. Phil took a gamble and made his way there, slipping into the crowded reception where he approached Buencamino's table. The doctor insisted he sit down, and introduced him to all his guests. Among them was Chief De LaFuente, head of the Manila Police.

Phil explained to Buencamino and De LaFuente about the unfortunate misunderstanding of his arrest. He said Attorney Teodoro believed the problem was just a misunderstanding that could be settled out of court. Then Phil explained his skip from police headquarters. Chief De LaFuente grew tight-lipped. It was the first he'd heard that a man in the custody of his detectives had waltzed.

Phil told them he planned next morning to put himself in the custody of Detective Olegario, a friend of Nena Nieto's brother. Attorney Teodoro would be there to assure that Phil's rights were respected.

Accompanied by Teodoro and Detective Olegario, Phil would be taken to the offices of the city prosecuting attorney, Fiscal Bengson, to discuss the fraud charges. Phil said he was confident Teodoro would present his case sympathetically to Bengson, so Phil would be released on bail. All Phil needed at this crucial moment from Dr. Buencamino was some backstage support. The doctor assured Phil he would take action at once. Chief De LaFuente also assured Phil he would "put in a good word".

In the genial ambiance of the Manila Hotel, the issue of bail was totally forgotten. Phil went to a friend's house to hide out till dawn.

The next morning, Phil dressed in a white sharkskin suit, figuring it would be a victorious day, so he and Nena could celebrate by going out on the town. Meeting Detective Olegario at a downtown restaurant, he was surprised that Attorney Teodoro was absent. Regardless, Olegario had his orders to bring Phil over to police headquarters.

When they arrived, Detective Salas and the rest of his department were lined up to welcome their escapee. Phil was finger-printed and booked for the second time in 48-hours. Apparently, Teodoro had forgotten his appointment with Phil, and Chief De LaFuente had forgotten to "put in a good word".

Feeling betrayed, Phil was taken to Cell Number Four of Bilibad Prison. During the war, the Japanese had used it as an execution chamber, burying their many victims in the prison grounds.

Getting to Cell Four involved negotiating a plank walkway across the exercise yard, knee-deep in mud and water from recent rains. In a corner of the exercise yard a hole serving as a communal toilet had overflowed. Cell Four was a rectangular concrete room fifteen feet by twenty. In daylight, prisoners were allowed to range between the cell and the exercise yard. At dusk they were herded into the cell and locked up.

Phil saw he was sharing the cell with seven men. Three were captured safe-crackers. The fourth, an Italian, had cooperated with the police, so he enjoyed the dubious privilege of spending each evening in a nearby women's holding cell crowded with women and girls of all ages, including more than a few off-duty prostitutes. The fifth and sixth prisoners were two pathetic Russians, who had pretended to be Soviet secret agents in an attempt to con people out of money. No formal charges had been brought against them, but once in Bilibad you were forgotten. They had been confined so long they were considered "veteran" inmates, so the Russians each had an iron bunk with a mattress, as a sign of seniority. The seventh prisoner was an American facing charges of drug-dealing. Dressed in his white sharkskin suit, Phil looked as out of place as a nun in a brothel.

He slept badly, and waited the whole next day for a bail hearing and release, which did not happen. Another night and day passed. He spent sleepless hours swapping stories with cellmates. The second morning he badgered the guards, telling them he had an appointment with Fiscal Bengson. They spat in his face, to get him to step back from the iron bars. Soon they quit paying attention. While haranguing them, Phil had used the grill's padlock as a lever, bending its old wire loop back and forth until it broke. Phil waved the broken wire in the air and shouted: "Look at me, I'm trying to escape!"

The nearest guard yelled at the top of his lungs, raising the alarm. Ignoring the plank walkway, the guard plunged through the mud soup of the courtyard, up to his knees, waving a pistol and spewing curses.

Phil's bravado evaporated. He had provoked a policeman, who had a gun, and was now covered with foul smelling mud. The guard had a lifetime of pent up hatred for everyone who insulted him. He took a wild swing and smacked the handle of his pistol against Phil's head.

Instinctively, Phil tried to cover his head and stomach as blows were repeated, then extended his arm to deflect a really nasty blow. The pistol connected with his wrist. Excruciating pain shot up his arm.

All hell broke loose. Whistles screamed as more guards poured into the fray, each one kicking or punching Phil who was trying to curl up in a fetal position on the cell floor. Like a pack of jackals, the guards' brutality inflicted as many injuries on their partners as on Phil.

Subdued, Phil's hands were cuffed and he was hauled by his cuffs through the mud, his white suit turning brown, to the main office. Bruised, bloody, and smelling real bad, Phil kept asking for Chief De LaFuente. After an hour, the Chief and Detective Olegario came in. The first prison guard, waving the broken wire and padlock, claimed that Phil had attacked him while trying to escape.

Chief De LaFuente expressed surprise, and regret, that Phil had not yet been taken to Fiscal Bengson. This must be done immediately. In the meantime, Phil was returned to Cell Four.

As a result of his antics, all the prisoners (with the exception of the Italian lothario) were now confined to the cell, without food or access to the shared latrine.

Phil was ostracized, a target of verbal abuse. Even the two Russians were openly hostile.

That night, the Italian returned from a tryst in the women's cell, and told Phil he had learned of a plan by the guards to fake an escape where Phil would be murdered. Next morning two detectives came to escort Phil to the Fiscal but, frightened by the Italian's warning, Phil refused to go.

The day dragged by. At supper time, a guard threw the raw rear end of a female caribou into the cell. The Italian, a comic by nature, tried to lighten the group tension by walking around the cell with the caribou's rump, exclaiming: "No need for me to visit the women's cell tonight." For Phil it was again a sleepless night, keeping one eye open.

Five days after being thrown into Cell Four, Phil's bail was arranged with payment of a bond of 1,000 pesos and he was released. His friend Gus Vallejo, of Philippine Air Lines, arranged the bail with Alto Bond and Surety Company. Gus and Jerry Widrin signed as guarantors. It was July 22, 1947.

Out of Bilibad, Phil had a long bath, then got in touch with Attorney Teodoro, who arranged a meeting with Fiscal Bengson the next day. Phil wanted Teodoro to make the point that he had only been an employee of JavaChina, and therefore was not responsible for company debts.

Teodoro argued instead for forgiveness, a no-contest plea, tantamount to pleading guilty. At first Phil rejected the idea cold, but Teodoro persuaded him it was the Filipino way.

However, when Teodoro put this no-contest plea to Fiscal Bengson the next day, the prosecutor realized he had Phil by the throat, and became wildly hostile. This case, he fumed, could only be settled in a Filipino court, judged by Filipinos. They would make an example of Phil. "Maybe we can't hold the U.S. responsible for their obligations, but you we can."

This outburst of hypocrisy -- punishing the weak for the crimes of the strong -- was a particular sorepoint to the hugely popular Dr. Buencamino, who wrote:

"It was the task of my generation, under the leadership of Quezon, to seek the independence of this country. Then came the war, and something snapped. It was patriotic to steal from the enemy; to sabotage him. The only trouble was that long after the war was over, the stealing orgy went on, not the least among those in positions of authority. The desire to possess material things became a pervasive obsession. The prewar brand of integrity seems to have been destroyed. Vote buying became more rampant. Terrorism reigned, often with the acquiescence of the men at the top. Quezon once said he'd rather have a government run like hell by the Filipinos than a government run like heaven by the Americans. It is a tragedy that a government run like hell came so soon."

Phil was stunned by Bengson's outburst. Teodoro had been misguided to think Phil should plead no contest to such a man. Powerful friends had let him down. He had been a fool to think he could win justice in a place with no justice even for its own citizens. He had no intention of going into a Manila Court.

Justice be damned. There was only one solution: escape, and to hell with the bail money posted on his behalf. And, for the moment, he was free on bail. In all of this, Cheez's fate out in Bataan had not once crossed his mind.

Chapter 18 :

BILIBAD AGAIN?

Once again Phil was disastrously wrong. He thought he was secure out on bail, and had plenty of time to make his escape with Jerry Widrin. But when word reached the Quirinos that bail had been granted, they took action immediately.

The next morning a bondsman from Alto Bond and Surety Company showed up at the LCM and told Phil the owner of Alto Bond ruled that neither Widrin nor Vallejo qualified as a guarantor. He said Phil had 24-hours to find more qualified guarantors, or his bond would be cancelled, and he would go back to Bilibad.

The bondsman followed him to Nena Nieto's house where, in desperation, Phil phoned Attorney Teodoro and Episcopal Bishop Norman Binsted, both of whom agreed to sign as new guarantors. The bondsman returned to his office, apparently satisfied, but Nena's phone soon rang.

The bondsman said Phil was to call Judge Quirino immediately because Teodoro did not qualify as a guarantor as he was Phil's lawyer, and Bishop Binsted had no property as collateral.

Call Judge Quirino?

Phil knew the name, of course, but never guessed that Tony 'The Fixer' Quirino was also the owner of Alto Bond, and one of the big thorns in Phil's paw from the very beginning.

He was not sure what "Call Judge Quirino" meant, but it smelled bad. Hoping to straighten out the bail issue, and stay out of Bilibad, he phoned as instructed and made an appointment to see Judge Quirino the following day. Both Jerry and Nena urged him to watch his back, to pay closer attention to danger signals. Mysterious forces were jerking his chain. There were thousands of unsolved murders in Manila each month. Taking his friends' advice seriously for a change, he asked former swimming champion Ben Salvador to accompany him to the meeting with Judge Tony. Salvador, a guy with bulging muscles who was afraid of nothing, rode on the Harley's pillion to watch Phil's back.

They were greeted unctuously by Judge Tony, who wore a thousand dollar Saville Row suit and a hand-sewn crocodile smile. Phil was hoping for advice about his bail.

Instead, after some throat-clearing, Judge Tony showed him the Filipino Sidestep. Evading the bail issue entirely, he told Phil he should ask for an immediate trial on the Estafa fraud charges, separate from the co-defendants, Cheez and Winkelman. In the oily manner practiced by morticians, Quirino explained that if all three were tried together, the guilt of one would smear the others.

As Winkelman was not in The Philippines, the Dutchman was safe. Quirino said that Cheez, being Russian, had no chance of a fair trial even in his own country. So Phil should take Quirino's advice and have his case heard separately. He even offered to prepare immediately a request for such a separate trial. Phil could pick up the document the next morning and deliver it personally to Judge DeLeon of the Court of First Instance, a good friend of Judge Tony. Phil left feeling great.

As arranged, next day Phil and Ben Salvador picked up the document at Quirino's office, in a large envelope secured with string and wax seals. He could not read what Quirino said without breaking the seals.

Leaving the Harley on the sidewalk and walking over to the courthouse, Phil handed the envelope to Judge DeLeon. The judge broke the seals, opened the envelope, scanned its contents. Not raising his eyes, he made a gesture. Two marshals appeared out of nowhere, handcuffed Phil, and put him in a courthouse holding cell. Instead of requesting a separate trial, Judge Tony had informed Judge DeLeon that Phil's bond had been canceled by Alto Bond, so he should be put back in Bilibad.

Phil had been tricked again, this time into delivering himself back to Bilibad Prison.

Handcuffed in a holding cell at the court house, he had no choice but to wait and see if any of his friends would come to his rescue. Ben Salvador had hurried off to alert Jerry Widrin.

Jerry Widrin alerted Nena Nieto, who contacted the American Embassy, and Bishop Binsted. Not that they would or could do anything.

The two marshals guarding his cell seemed to be very nice, sharing chocolate bars with him. They said they would take him to Bilibad at the end of their work day, at 5 p.m. To seem friendly and easy-going in return, Phil offered to pay for a full tank of gas for the marshals' Jeep.

Meanwhile, he stir-fried a getaway plan.

"My biggest fear was getting shot by one marshal while subduing the other, so I planned to separate them. I had told Ben Salvador to have a friend move my motorcycle from directly in front of the courthouse entrance, to a spot about 100 feet down the sidewalk. When we left for Bilibad, I would ask one of the marshals to move my cycle through a gate to a safe place inside the municipal compound, where it could not be stolen. While he was doing that, I'd just have only one marshal to cope with."

Shortly after 5:00 p.m., the two marshals reappeared as promised, and took Phil out of the holding cell. As they escorted him out of the courthouse entrance, on their way to a Jeep, Phil called their attention to his Harley parked on the public sidewalk some distance away, where it could easily be stolen, and asked if one of them would please move it inside the compound for safekeeping.

Instead, both marshals walked toward the Harley with Phil sandwiched between them. When they got to the bike, one marshal tried to move it.

The bike was too heavy for the small man, and fell over on its side. Crying out in alarm, as if the bike was badly damaged, Phil grabbed the handlebars, righted the bike, and sat on the seat. Pointing to old scars and dents, he feigned shock over the 'damage'. Warily, one of the marshals backed off, placing his hand on his gun.

"I assured him everything was okay, that this was the best way to keep the Harley upright, while pushing it down the sidewalk and through the gate. I started pushing and they pitched in, dropping their guard. We were leaning into it, grunting and pushing as hard as we could but getting nowhere, because I had slipped the transmission into low gear. Feathering the clutch and brake, I was maintaining enough resistance to make it nearly impossible to move the very heavy motorcycle. After fifty feet, both marshals were exhausted. I pretended to be, as well. I suggested that I start the bike to coast the rest of the way to the open gate. Without waiting for a reply, I started the engine. Both men looked astonished, then relaxed as I inched the bike toward the gate.

"A bus was approaching. I cranked the handlebars left and poured gas into the motor. The Harley shot off the two-foot curb directly in front of the bus. I nearly lost control, but knew I was shielded by the bus from any gunshots. I roared out Taft Avenue away from town. Hearing sirens, I took back streets to the Episcopal Church rectory.

There I was welcomed inside by Bishop Binsted and his wife.

"Foremost in my mind was that Detective Salas would be hellbent on getting me back in custody, where my chances of survival would be slim. Bishop Binsted urged me to return to the U.S. immediately, and thought it foolhardy to do otherwise. However, Winkelman still owed me money, and I wasn't going home empty-handed. First thing was to escape fast. Second was to get to Shanghai."

Bishop Binsted phoned friends who were pilots at Cathay Pacific Airways, in those days only a charter cargo airline. Leaving the rectory next morning, after a righteous sleep, Phil rode his Harley to their address.

The fantasy of taking the LCM to Borneo was now grudgingly put out of his mind. Everybody knew that was the plan, because Phil had told everybody.

"The pilots really were friendly. They said they would hide me in the rudder quadrant of their PBY flying boat until the Customs inspection was finished, then I could come forward to sit with them when we took off. But after a few days hiding out with them, the newspapers carried a story that police were narrowing their search for me to a particular neighborhood. I had to get out of Manila fast. I only had my portable typewriter, the clothes on my back, and my .32 Webley automatic. I strapped the typewriter on the Harley and, in darkness and warm rain, rode to another part of town where I took refuge with the girlfriend of the guy who had loaned Widrin and me the submachine gun.

"Francis put me up over a week while I grew a new mustache and she waved my hair to disguise me."

He then moved to the house of Nena's friend, Babs Lamoglia, who was employed as a secretary at Clark Air Base.

"Babs told me she had access to all the U.S. Army's official forms and could type up false travel orders for me. I could then put on my ATC officer's uniform, and try to get out on an Army flight. I knew plane crews just turned a blind eye. So, next morning, in my old uniform, I strapped my typewriter to the Harley again and headed for Clark, just north of Manila.

"Entering the base without difficulty in my uniform, I met Babs at her workplace and looked over the Travel Orders she had prepared. I chickened out right then when it sank in that I would be leaving a paper trail of carbon copies all over the Pacific, and could end up in Leavenworth, instead of Bilibad."

Phil wandered over to the base canteen for a soda, and tried being open and frank with a couple of young officers he met there, hoping they would help. Instead, one slipped out and sounded the alarm.

"I was seized by MPs for impersonating an officer, my Harley was impounded and, after beating the hell out of me, I was thrown into another holding cell at the air base. Word got out, and the following morning, Manila Police asked the U.S. Army to turn me over. If they ever got their hands on me, I was dead. My American jailers wrote me off as a nut, and ignored my requests that they phone Bishop Binsted. I was allowed to make one call. So I phoned Babs, who called others. Word spread and by noon I was released from the holding cell, but ordered not to leave the base. That was fine with me."

American GIs regarded the Manila Police with scorn. When detectives came to the gate at Clark to demand Phil's return, they were refused with suitable hand signals. As Phil's version of the truth made the rounds, base officials began to recognize that he was being victimized by a system they all knew was corrupt. Phil still worried that the U.S. Army headquarters in Honolulu or Washington might take the matter out of Clark's hands. They were unlikely to do that simply because he had impersonated an officer, which happened all the time.

Other Allied military forces also were based at Clark. As word of Phil's escapade spread, an Australian non-com asked him to come see his commanding officer. In another section of the air base, secluded from Yankees, he was introduced to a handsome and feisty Australian in Royal Air Force uniform. With a twinkle in his eye, Commander Keating said he had heard about Phil's dilemma.

Not everybody at Clark marched to the same tune, he said. There was 'a bit of rivalry' between the Allies, and he wouldn't mind interfering. Pointing to a plane on the tarmac, Keating asked with a grin, "How would you like to just disappear, Mate?"

An answering grin spread across Phil's face: "I'd like that just fine."

This was not merely inter-service rivalry. General MacArthur's arrogant manner throughout the war, his obvious contempt for everyone outside his inner circle, and his disregard for Allied casualties, infuriated the British, the Australians, and the New Zealanders. There had been some nasty incidents in Australia during the war that had gone unreported. Now that MacArthur was America's viceroy of the Pacific, he listened to no one but God -- and then only while having eye-contact in a mirror.

The RAF maintained a regular mail route from Clark Field to Japan by way of Okinawa. The plane on the airstrip was leaving shortly with bags of mail and two Roman Catholic Cardinals from Spain as courtesy passengers. Commander Keating said there was room for Phil.

"Keating introduced me to two Australian pilots who shook my hand and escorted me to the plane. As we were about to board, Keating told me the first stop would be Okinawa. I asked him to contact a friend of mine stationed there, Captain Connie Frank, and let him know I was on my way."

When they landed in Okinawa, the plane was met by a U.S. Army command car with a star on its door.

Phil's pal Captain Frank was now commanding officer of the Air Transport Service on the island. In the early days after the war, Phil and Connie had done each other favors. Phil had helped Connie get his hands on wristwatches, fountain pens, and other baubles he could take to China without customs inspections.

Under arrest at Clark only hours earlier, Phil was now treated as a VIP, hosted by one of the Okinawa base commanders. The next day, when Phil was reported missing at Clark, Connie Frank quickly had friends fly the dangerous fugitive to Nanking. From there he was flown by other military aircraft to Hong Kong, then to Shanghai, a trail nobody would be able to follow. It was mid-August.

After nearly a month at the mercy of Sergeant Salas and the Quirino brothers, Phil had been lucky to survive his own repeated folly. There had been no time even to think about Cheez, and all the allegations about his being a Soviet agent. Phil had no idea where Cheez was -- he'd simply vanished over in Bataan. Now that Phil was safe in Shanghai, he would try to get Winkelman to rescue Cheez.

Phil had been living a pipe-dream.

"Sure, later I realized I made some pretty crazy decisions and went off half-cocked more than once. Guess that's why we're strong enough to suffer through our twenties."

It would be many years before Phil grasped that more than bad-luck had been behind the persistent problems of the past 14 months. He did have a better idea who had been tripping them up, starting with Colonel Nieto, Vice President Quirino, and unidentified people at G-2. They were the Big Fish. The Lapu-Lapu. Their henchmen were MadDog Mabini, Captain Dimuahuan, Captain Vilamor. He was now alarmed about what might befall Cheez. He knew Winkelman blamed Cheez for mishandling business expenses in Manila. But Winkelman was only a neurotic businessman, not a deliberate trouble-maker. While in Bilibad with only his small portable typewriter to keep him busy, Phil had written a blunt letter to Winkelman:

"Here I am in cell number four, Bilibad Prison, bearing the obligations of a company which has forgotten that I exist. I didn't mind sharing financial losses, jeopardizing my life occasionally, and sacrificing what a little money can offer, as long as I could expect some restitution for my trouble. However, right now, here sits a once happy-go-lucky, carefree kid, who has now just about lost all faith in human nature. Like you have in the past, no doubt you can again compose a sarcastic letter, explaining my predicament as self-inflicted, etc., and even justify the action you have taken. However, I wonder if you or anyone else in Shanghai will ever be aware of exactly how much I've gone through, and for what? With no aid from you, my eventual jailing was inevitable. I've never hesitated to tell you my position, so don't this time act surprised.

Anticipating the present state of affairs, I attempted to leave the country several weeks ago, on the LCM, but the local authorities apprehended me, in view of the many pending cases against JavaChina, and created false charges of gun-running to hold me

until action could be taken by your creditors. I was arrested, brought here to the prison, but soon managed to escape.

The charges brought against me, and also the fellow who purchased the LCM from Cheez and me, which I enclose with this letter, are an example of so-called Philippine justice. However, after the Fiscal had completed the Estafa case against you, Cheez, and me, and warrants for our arrests were issued, this alleged gun-smuggling case was dropped. I was captured today, so it now seems like I have to face even more serious charges than before. Around here, Estafa is considered quite a serious charge. I have but 1,000 pesos in the LCM now. Anyway, I realize by now that it is futile to bother you either with statistics, or my troubles, so somehow or another I intend to get out of this hole.

When I do, I'm coming to Shanghai to visit you boys, and if damn good explanations are not forthcoming, people around the office are going to think all hell broke loose. Running around Manila with the burden of corporate debts, plus several thousands in personal debts, reduced me first to a pauper, then a fugitive, and now a convict. This has had a slight tendency to make me bitter."

Phil's letter sheds light on the argument raging for months between Shanghai and Manila about difficulties with the U.S. Army, the Seaman's Union, and cash flow. Phil saw that Winkelman simply did not care what happened to them -- that was their problem. Whatever went awry, he did not want to know.

When Winkelman replied from San Francisco, he was almost conciliatory, despite some body-blows: "I appreciate what you have tried to do, and for the way you have apparently risked your life and safety while protecting our common interests. It is, however, quite clear that neither you nor Chirskoff will ever be businessmen, or capable to run anything by yourselves. ... I have instructed Dr. Samet to pay you no more than US$100 per month until my return to Shanghai, at which time I will make some settlement with you myself."

Until that time came, Phil stayed out of sight at the Shanghai YMCA, wearing his old ATC officer's uniform when he went out so he would not be stopped casually by the Shanghai police. He saw a lot of Peterson and his bride. Pete urged him to stay in Asia and join him working for the UN Fishing Rehabilitation Administration, paying $900 a month, plus quarters and living expenses.

Phil urged Winkelman repeatedly to help Cheez: "The Philippines are a rough place to be in trouble. Although I'm out of danger now, Cheez is not. He doesn't deserve the fate in store for him if he is convicted.

"I'm trying to get the [Estafa] charges dropped but there's little hope as Cheez is the only 'collateral' for [JavaChina's] debts in Manila."

Winkelman stubbornly insisted that Cheez owed JavaChina over US$30,000: "You can do all the negotiating you want, but JCTC is not going to pay another penny to Manila or to Chirskoff. ... As far as I am concerned... they can keep Chirskoff in jail for another 50,000 years, I just don't care a damn."

Chapter 19 :

GRILLED CHEEZ

While Phil was in Bilibad Prison, Cheez was completely out of touch at Iman Point on the west coast of Bataan, struggling to make a go of logging. G-2 continued to watch him closely through the mayor and police chief at Morong. Once, when flat broke, Cheez came to Manila from Bataan hoping to borrow a few hundred pesos from Max Zalevsky. When Zalevsky refused, Cheez almost gave up -- nearly surrendered to G-2.

He imagined that he could get Lucero to block the phony Estafa charges, and the absurd charge of being a Soviet agent. Then all that remained would be the petty charge of overstaying his visa. Many G-2 agents had urged Cheez to become an informer within the Russian emigre community in Manila. He had often jokingly suggested it himself, to demonstrate that he was not a Kremlin spy.

But Lansdale and Bohannan knew he was not a spy. They were using Cheez as false evidence of an 'imminent communist threat' to make the pathetically impoverished Huks look like Marxist maniacs trying to overthrow the owners of the brothel.

G-2 files show they also had been watching Winkelman and Samet closely. They knew that Phil had considered taking JavaChina to court in Shanghai's International Settlement, over the Estafa issue. However, G-2's motives had nothing to do with reality, The charge of fraud always was as fake as the charge of gunrunning, despite being splashed all over the Manila newspapers. The legal records show that no charges of any kind were ever filed in Philippine courts against Phil, Pete, or Cheez. The Big Fish never intended to collect back wages claimed by captains and crews. The prime motive of Lansdale and Bohannan was simply to advance their careers as Grand Inquisitors in the postwar anti-communist witch-hunts, while reinforcing the 'urgent' need for 'containment' and death-squads. Sadly, though, this would never make headlines, and their utterly false allegation that Cheez was a Russian agent would vaporize the moment he was humiliated and destroyed. Meantime, he was Lansdale's catnip mouse.

By the end of July, when Phil fled to Clark Field, Cheez was nowhere to be found. Searching for him in Bataan failed, because G-2 looked only at Iman Point and Morong. At first they wondered whether he had successfully slipped out of the country like Phil. In fact, Cheez was still in Bataan, but looking for work farther up the peninsula. He had given up on the Iman Point logging operation. Men he hired from Morong were nothing but trouble, and he could not afford professional loggers like the Visayans who had worked for Phil.

At first Cheez got work hauling logs out of the forest with his two remaining bulldozers. When he became sick, his largest bulldozer was stolen. Later, the other would also be stolen.

Eventually, he found manual labor for Chinese loggers at wages that barely kept skin and bone together. Moving from logging camp to logging camp, he drifted out of the Bataan mountains into foothills closer to Pampanga. On forest trails he sometimes encountered small bands of ragged armed men he assumed might be Huks.

They hardly seemed to be 'true disciples of Marx'.

Not a day passed when bodies were not seen floating in the rivers, or strewn by roadsides. Valeriano's 'Nenita' death-squads were roaring around Central Luzon with skull-and-crossbones flags flying from their jeeps and scout cars, looking for victims of all ages. Their cruelty and lust for murder were psychotic. A Filipino senator wrote to President Roxas demanding the removal of Valeriano from Pampanga, "for having committed many atrocities, not only against dissident elements but against law-abiding people." The 'skull-squadrons' rarely took prisoners, usually shooting whoever they stopped in the back of the head. Whether or not they were Huks did not matter. The Nenita wasted no time with legal procedures or even interrogation.

In return the Huks, who had learned to fight under brutal Japanese occupation, treated captured Military Police with equal viciousness.

Bohannan and Valeriano then demanded mutilation of bodies. They introduced a new weapon in their terror campaign: two ice-picks taped together and used to stab villagers in the throat, leaving what looked like vampire bite-marks in a horror movie. Ghoulish stories of vampires were spread across the countryside, of which these mutilation killings were evidence.

During those months, Cheez made so little money that he often went hungry, suffering a series of small heart attacks that frightened him.

In October, G-2 investigators reported: "Mrs. Chirskoff, who is still in Shanghai, has become somewhat anxious in regard to her husband's safety, as even she has been without word from him for some time."

In December, the mischievous plywood salesman Zalevsky told G-2 that Cheez was "without finances and under pressure to return to Russia." This, he clearly hoped, would play into G-2's fantasy that Cheez really was working directly for Moscow.

Captain Lucero informed G-2 that Cheez had spent a bleak Christmas in Lucero's home. He had found Cheez walking down a Manila street in bad condition, his clothes shabby, like some desperate character from a Joseph Conrad novel, rejected by the world and by himself.

Lucero scooped Cheez up, took him home, fed him, and insisted that he spend the holidays with the family. Whatever else, Lucero was far more compassionate about Cheez's personal health and situation than was Winkelman.

"At the time [Lucero reported], subject had obviously been sick, and seemed in very bad condition in general, as well as broke. According to subject, he has been sick a long time, and while sick the remnants of his property were stolen from him, so he no longer even has his tractors or motorcycle." Lucero gave Cheez a bundle of letters that had arrived in care of Mrs. Lucero. "Letters received from his wife in Shanghai seen by informant were pathetic, consisting of pleas for money and descriptions of their suffering. Subject borrowed twenty pesos from informant, and stated that he was returning to Bataan." (At least Cheez was prudent enough to tell Lucero he was returning to Bataan, not to Pampanga.)

Incredibly, after showing such compassion, Lucero reported that he believed Cheez was "sent here [to The Philippines] as an espionage agent by the USSR, but was cut off the payroll." Lucero knew perfectly well that it had been Winkelman, the capitalist, who had cut Cheez off his payroll.

Cheez had only one real friend in The Philippines. This was Esperanza, the homely and gentle maid Cheez had hired to look after Georgie at the Manila Hotel and to manage the rented house on Roberts Road for Nina. As her name meant Hope, he was literally clinging to

Hope. In that winter of 1947-1948, working at a mill in Pampanga, he wrote to her:

"**Dear Esperanza, I received your letter but did not write until now as I expected to be in Manila before the end of Feb. However, since I'll not have the time to see you before the 7/8 of the month I am writing this. If you will write to me do not address your letter to the P.S.M. or Mr. Jasper anymore, but use the following address: V.N. Cheez (And not Chirskoff) c/o S. DIZON, Florida Blanca, Pampanga. Do not give my address to anybody at all. If there is any mail for me send it down. If you have some of my clothes at your place send the same by Parcel Post or something like that. Do not come yourself. I want to see you pretty badly myself and sometimes I miss your company very badly. Take care of yourself -- see you soon. Your friend, V. N. C.**"

Chapter 20 :

ENDGAME

Six days after writing to Esperanza, Cheez was arrested by the Philippine Constabulary, the military police with authority in rural areas outside Manila. No one could avoid Lansdale's Egyptian Magic Eye. Esperanza may have unwarily shown Cheez' letter to Lucero, who was both a Lansdale snoop and an officer of the Constabulary, However it happened, Esperanza was mortified.

Cheez recalled later that "on Sat. 6th of March came along two Philippine Constabulary agents and informed me that I was, or supposed to be, a Huk contact man ...and took me to the Immigration Authorities who put me in the City Jail [at Florida Blanca]. I was held incommunicado."

Specifically, he was arrested in a village or 'barrio' called Carmencita where he was living just outside Florida Blanca. G-2 files indicate that he was badly beaten during six days of interrogations at Florida Blanca. Cheez does not mention the beatings.

The warrant for his arrest, issued by Immigration Commissioner Engracio Fabre on the 28th of February 1948, asserted that Cheez was a contact man for the Huk guerillas.

The Manila press jumped all over the story, after being hand-fed the facts by G-2. All the papers said Cheez was heard "inciting the peasants and Huks" to take up arms against the government of The Philippines; that he was giving aid and comfort to the 'dissident elements', and was smuggling arms and ammunition into Huk camps.

Having lost track of Cheez for many months, this was Lansdale's first public bodyblow to his victim. Cheez was Lansdale's 'most prized' non-Filipino target in a long list of people he tormented or had murdered in the course of an extraordinary career as a Cold Warrior. Lansdale assured the Manila newspapers that Cheez was unquestionably a Soviet spy. Not just an illiterate peasant, but "an honest-to-god Stalinist secret agent sent by the Kremlin". He knew all along that this simply was not true.

Significantly, there was no mention in the arrest warrant that Cheez was guilty of Estafa. Those allegations had vaporized. During his week-long interrogations, Cheez told the truth about what had happened to him in The Philippines. He was so ill and exhausted that nothing would be gained by being contrary. He no longer had the energy to be defiant. The dossier quotes Cheez about how he was methodically destroyed:

"Ever since I delivered the last ship out of The Philippines, [JavaChina] stopped all financial help and I was forced with my friend Mr. Mehan ... to look to some business as a form of livelihood. We secured tractors, mostly on credit, and started operations.

"Not knowing the business, we were cheated right and left; finally just before rainy season we were the victims of an armed robbery and most of our equipment was lost. Mr. Mehan left as he was tired of the lumber business and wanted to go to Borneo with some friends of his. I tried working in an adjoining concession ...but the rainy season plus the impossible terrain made it very difficult. [I] met a Chinese lumber dealer by the name of Siha from Baceler, Pampanga and he was interested to have our tractor work down in Florida Blanca ... Everything went along fine until we started asking this Chinaman for [payment] and found out he was operating on a shoestring and had no money at all. Finally ... we gave up. ... [Later] in conjunction with the owner of the concession, Mr. Leon Dizon at whose house I was staying in Florida Blanca, [and I] started to work it again. We were starting to do quite well when I was suddenly arrested. ... My name has been blasted and blackened in the press. No charges up to date have been pressed against me."

After the week of rough interrogation, he was transferred to a detention cell of the Bureau of Immigration in Manila, where he was questioned further. They played stick and carrot with him: "I was only informed yesterday that I could put up a bond of cash, which I do not have as my money comes in small sums from pulling logs... I am offered voluntary deportation as it seems there is nothing against me, and have come to the conclusion that it's better to accept all this and get out of The Philippines than rot in jail without any hope of fairness or justice.

"It seems to me that if you're a Russian you're a very low animal that has no rights and should be just stamped upon by anybody who is not afraid of dirtying his foot."

Finally, addressing specific allegations in the warrant, Cheez stated: "As regards the Huks ... I readily admitted [to Commissioner Fabre] having seen these characters on several occasions ... but requested him to keep [this] confidential as this information had already been passed to authorities in Florida Banca, to the Sgt of Police Gregorie Dizon and the Chief of Police [and] PC agents, and must be kept confidential ... for the sake of my safety... However, the next day I read all about it in the Press. Maybe the Commissioner did not want those Huks apprehended? ... I was willing to do a little investigating in this line but will definitely not anymore as I would most certainly be murdered for my efforts. The information regarding me secured by Philippine Constabulary officers in Florida Blanca was only that I had always cooperated with the Police and the P.C., even to the extent of providing information and trucks for their raids."

Not only was he innocent, but at the time of his arrest he was actually living in the home of the police sergeant of Florida Blanca, Gregorie Dizon, keeping the sergeant and the chief of police informed whenever he saw small groups of Huks passing on trails in the rainforest. In that region, everyone had to have police passes to travel outside their village by foot, and Cheez had such a pass so he could work with Leon Dizon -- father of the police sergeant.

People who left their villages without a pass were shot dead on the spot by Lansdale's death squads. As he was working with the sergeant's father, on a pass from the sergeant, and living in the sergeant's house, how could Cheez possibly be busy "encouraging the Huks to overthrow the government", and "supplying them with weapons and ammunition"?

None of the charges made sense. But this was The Philippines, on Lansdale's watch, when everything became surreal.

Only once following his arrest did Cheez lose his composure, when he protested the way the government had hounded him for no reason:

"During my stay at the Manila Hotel, I was constantly under surveillance of different agents of the Philippine government who even went so far as to inform all the guests in the Manila Hotel that I was a Russian agent. I was awfully mad about this and visited several agencies like the MPC, Philippine Army, U.S. Army, etc., and offered to answer any questions they cared to ask and requested that the men concerned should not be so insulting in their manner of searching my wastepaper basket."

This affidavit was written and signed by Cheez on March 12, 1948, in a holding cell at Immigration, where he continued to be interrogated until March 16.

All Cheez's affidavits and transcripts of his interrogations were carefully reviewed by Bohannan, and an 'interpretive' summary about "this communist ring" was written by him for his G-2 superiors in Manila, Tokyo, and Washington.

Bohannan's most significant conclusion was that Filipino police and secret service agents could not be trusted to keep their mouths shut. He noted that they had stupidly shown Cheez and Phil the six-inch thick G-2 dossier on their "communist activities", violating the basic rule of a secret investigation -- to remain secret. Whether or not you have a case against someone, or evidence to support your case, reveal nothing. Bohannan concluded that Filipino detectives were incompetent.

Despite utter lack of evidence, Cheez was first arrested on March 6, beaten for a week at the local jail, transferred to an Immigration holding cell in Manila on March 12 for further beatings and interrogations, then according to official records of the Manila Court was 'formally' arrested on March 16, when he was moved to Bilibad Prison.

Even after locking him up in Bilibad, no formal charges were preferred against Cheez. Although the warrant for his arrest had alleged that he had supplied weapons and ammunition to the Huks, those allegations never became formal charges, yet Cheez was made to disappear in Bilibad to rot his life away.

Chapter 21 :

DISAPPEARED

Cheez remained in prison from March 1948 until October 1951. No formal charges were ever brought against him by the Philippine government, or U.S. counter-intelligence. He was simply imprisoned all those years on suspicion. In wretched cells, with disgusting food, he read novels lent to him by prison wardens, and waged a solitary battle for his freedom, fruitlessly trying first one approach, then another.

He remained in legal limbo until one day Claro Recto, one of The Philippines' most famous attorneys, turned him into an international legal celebrity of sorts, showing Lansdale and G-2 to be malicious buffoons. As a direct consequence, Claro Recto would be tracked secretly for years by the enraged Lansdale, who finally got his revenge when he had Recto poisoned during a trip to Rome in 1960. By that time Lansdale was one of the CIA's top Cold Warriors, actively plotting the assassination of Fidel Castro, with access to a pharmacy of poisons that could make murder look like a heart attack. It unfolded this way:

Cheez had been rotting in prison for more than a year when in April 1948 President Roxas died suddenly after delivering a speech at Clark Air Base. While his death was attributed to a heart attack, the circumstances were so unusual and the timing so curious that foul play was never in question. Insiders concluded that he was the victim of Vice President Quirino, who moved up a notch into Malacanang Palace. As President, Quirino began to assert his independence of Washington and his role as strongman of a newly independent country. Washington concluded that Quirino was only trying to extort bigger sums in foreign aid, and in U.S. rent for the continued use of Clark and Subic bases. CIA Director Allen Dulles offered Lansdale $5-million to block Quirino's re-election by whatever means necessary. Quirino then began to exhibit health problems. Some thought he was becoming senile because his speech was slurred and he stumbled a lot. In fact, Lansdale had conspired with the CIA's Manila station chief, General Ralph B. Lovett, to feed Quirino drugs that made him look debilitated and incompetent.

While this waltz was being danced, Cheez appealed directly to Immigration Commissioner Fabre to simply expel him from The Philippines.

Lansdale and Bohannan wanted to avoid this at all cost. Cheez was their only smoking gun, their only 'evidence' they could cite to justify their claim that the Huks were being supported by Moscow. So Lansdale visited Commissioner Fabre and bullied him into participating in a public relations spectacle modeled on the U.S. House Un-American Activities Committee (HUAC). HUAC had got its start in the mid-1930s, investigating Nazi and Soviet propaganda inside the United States.

After the Nazi defeat in 1945, HUAC focused exclusively on Communists and 'fellow travelers'.

One committee member famously asked a witness whether Elizabethan playwright Christopher Marlowe had been a member of the Communist Party.

Senator Joe McCarthy went on a rampage of accusations that destroyed the careers of government officials, diplomats, scientists, and more than 300 artists—film directors, radio commentators, actors and screenwriters. Some, like Charlie Chaplin, left the U.S. for good. In most cases, only allegations were necessary to doom the person named.

Lansdale persuaded cooperative Filipino congressmen to create the House Un-Filipino Activities Committee of the Philippine Congress. Its public hearings started in October 1948, with Commissioner Fabre handpicked by Lansdale as the first witness, and Cheez as the star villain.

Fabre testified: "Communistic tendencies among aliens here will spread unless the government takes [action]." Especially Russian secret agents aiding the Huk rebellion.

Fabre said four Russians rounded up recently and ordered to be deported were still in Philippine prisons because the skipper of a Russian ship had refused to take them aboard.

Shanghai authorities also refused to accept them.

Fabre got lurid press coverage when he declared that one of the four imprisoned Russians, Vadim Nicolaevich Chriskoff [sic], "threatened to come back here as a two-star general".

Fabre could not avoid acting as Lansdale's mouthpiece because Bohannan had learned that Fabre was operating his own Immigration Department racket, extorting big payments from people who overstayed their visas.

Fabre did try several times to deport Cheez. G-2 files note that Fabre was desperate "to see Chirskoff out of The Philippines". The Commissioner sent word to Cheez that he would be allowed out of Bilibad a few hours each day so he could look for a berth on any foreign freighter in Manila harbor. For weeks, Cheez visited shipping companies, and ships in the harbor. Eventually, he found a berth on a Swedish freighter, the SS AXEL SALEM, but when Lansdale and Bohannan heard about it, they forced Fabre to renege on the deal, returning Cheez to the bowels of Bilibad Prison. The commissioner backpedalled furiously.

"Fabre stated that Chirskoff had attempted to persuade him to allow him to return to Shanghai at his own expense. ... Fabre stated that he had communicated with Chinese officials on the question of Chirskoff's return and that the Chinese ... had refused to consider it. [Then] Chirskoff ... tried to persuade Mr. Fabre to let [him] buy a boat and sail it to Vladivostok. Mr. Fabre refused because he was afraid [Chirskoff] would just sail to some other part of The Philippines."

Fabre's blood must have run cold when Bohannan "suggested that ... he be permitted to interview Chirskoff privately and attempt to extract additional information from him as a price for his departure."

Even Fabre could not wish that on another human being. For blocking Bohannan's interrogation of Cheez, Fabre was removed from his post.

Throughout this dismal misadventure, Cheez was surprisingly calm. His life in one of the world's most dismal prisons had become monotonously routine. He was able to receive and send mail. He corresponded with Jerry Widrin, Phil Mehan, and others, describing his life in prison. Writing to Phil in Shanghai, he said:

"I've not heard back from Jerry at all ... he promised to write for sure and tell me what the deal was [with JavaChina regarding Cheez's back salary], but not even a note. ... I hope Gus won't be afraid of writing to me. How's Samet making out? ...were you able to collect more from them? It's pretty late right now, the place is silent as a morgue, except for the tortured cries of the sleeping Muslims [prisoners from Mindanao]. ... I sure could write an interesting book."

He exhibited only one trace of bitterness, reserved for Winkelman. "I just hope that bastard Winkelman passes thru The Philippines. If he does intend to, let me know."

A knee-capping, or worse, could be arranged.

In letters, he informed Phil about his efforts to get out. After losing his first plea for release on habeas corpus, he filed a petition to the Filipine Supreme Court. "I have no lawyer and do my own petitioning with the help of a law book or two. The man who did a great deal in helping me (the Director of Prisons) died a week ago and now as far as getting things expedited, I am on my own. I have no hopes, only dreams."

Violent events then changed the rules of habeas corpus in the islands. On April 28, 1949, the widow of prewar President Manuel Quezon was on her way by car through the Sierra Madre mountains to inaugurate the Quezon Memorial Hospital in her home town of Baler, the same town where Cheez had befriended the mayor. In the car, she was accompanied by her eldest daughter, and son-in-law. Mrs. Quezon was hugely popular as a 'queen-mother and patron saint'. She still had political leverage that she used against the Quirinos. According to press reports, the small motorcade was "ambushed by 210 Huks under the leadership of Commander Stalin" -- a name dreamed up by Lansdale. Mrs. Quezon, her daughter and son-in-law, all died. The outpouring of grief over their death, blamed on the Huks, made it easy for President Quirino to shut down civil rights in October 1950 by declaring martial law, suspending habeas corpus throughout the country. TIME magazine quoted a Philippine Congressman saying that suspension of habeas corpus was "less to ferret out Communists than to intimidate Quirino critics."

So long as martial law remained in effect, Cheez had no chance of being released. He could only hope that some day his predicament would become known to "a person with power and a sense of justice". This took human form in the person of Claro Recto, an attorney with long experience in the Philippine House of Representatives, and as an associate justice in the Supreme Court.

A small group of Filipino reformers were trying to pull the country out of the sewer. They decided to make an issue of the persecution of Cheez and other White Russian refugees in the islands. In this circle,

Claro Recto was regarded by American and Philippine intelligence agents as particularly 'dangerous' because he was a genuine nationalist, who wanted to get America completely out of The Philippines.

He also intended to see that guarantees provided by the Philippine Constitution were upheld.

In the controlled press Recto was tarred as a Japanese collaborator -- the same press that exonerated Quirino and the late President Roxas of the same charge. While they were straw-dog nationalists, Recto was the real thing -- an enemy of the superstate. He said Philippine independence was an illusion, because American hegemony was now more deeply entrenched than ever. The Philippine government still allowed Americans to dominate the financial, commercial, and industrial life of the country. Huge sums paid to Manila as foreign aid, and as rent for the military bases, was payola that vanished into the hands of the oligarchs, keeping them as dependent and submissive as drug addicts.

Cheez had no idea that Recto was pressing his case. The two men never met. One was in the high court, the other in Bilibad.

Finally, in 1951, when Cheez had been in prison for four years without charges or trial, Recto managed to get his petition heard by the Supreme Court of The Philippines. The Supreme Court's decision set a landmark precedent in Filipino criminal and constitutional law that remains on the books to this day.

The Court's judgment was given on October 26, 1951:

G.R. No. L-3802
VADIM N. CHIRSKOFF, petitioner, vs.
COMMISSIONER OF IMMIGRATION
and DIRECTOR OF PRISONS, respondents.

Claro M. Recto for petitioner.

[The decision begins with a brief summary of Cheez's misadventures in The Philippines:]

"The history of the prisoner's detention is thus set forth in the petition: Chirskoff entered The Philippines on June 11, 1946, with a passport duly visaed by the United States Consul in Shanghai, for the purpose of making repairs on and taking delivery of certain vessels purchased by or in behalf of the Java China Trading Co., Ltd. The vessels having been repaired and dispatched to Shanghai, the petitioner remained behind and stayed for the reason, according to him, that he had "suffered an economic collapse and his return to Shanghai became impracticable.""

[The circumstances of Cheez's arrest were then given:]

"In the meantime Chirskoff obtained employment in a lumber concern in Bataan and later in a similar concern in Floridablanca, Pampanga. It was while working at the latter place that he was arrested by order of the Commissioner of Immigration on March 16, 1948, charged with aiding, helping and promoting 'the final objective of the Hukbalahaps to overthrow the Government.' ...No formal charges for giving aid to Hukbalahaps have ever been filed."

[Cheez's efforts to get out of The Philippines are then mentioned:]

"The petitioner repeatedly expressed his desire to leave the country on his own account but that his request was not heeded. The petitioner says that he could easily have departed from The Philippines without any expense on the part of the Government when, upon press authority of the respondent Commissioner of Immigration, he secured employment in the which was to sail from The Philippines in 1948, but, so he states, the respondent Commissioner of Immigration for no valid and practical reason withdrew the said authority."

[The unlawfulness of Cheez's detention is then made clear:]

"Foreign nationals, not enemy, against whom no criminal charges have been formally made or judicial order issued, may not indefinitely be kept in detention; that in the 'Universal Declaration of Human Rights' approved by the General Assembly of the United Nations of which The Philippines is a member, the right to life and liberty and all other fundamental rights as applied to human beings were proclaimed."

JUDGEMENT AND TERMS OF RELEASE

"It is ordered that the writ issue commanding the respondents to release the petitioner from custody upon these terms: The petitioner shall be placed under the surveillance of the immigration authorities or their agents in such form and manner as may be deemed adequate to insure that he keep peace and be available when the Government is ready to deport him. The surveillance shall be reasonable and the question of reasonableness shall be submitted to this Court or to the Court of First Instance of Manila for decision in case of abuse. He shall also put up a bond for the above purpose in the amount of P5,000 with sufficient surety or sureties, which bond the Commissioner of Immigration is authorized to exact."

Recto's victory provoked homicidal rage in the U.S. intelligence services, particularly in the CIA and the Pentagon, whose base-leases at Clark and Subic were constantly threatened by popular resistance to American interference in Filipino life. So, Recto must be punished.

When Recto ran for President in the 1957 national elections, the CIA distributed tens of thousands of perforated condoms marked "Courtesy of Claro M. Recto -- the People's Friend." Recto lost the election.

Revenge then moved beyond dirty-tricks. Lansdale's friend, General Lovett, CIA station chief in Manila, and U.S. Ambassador Admiral

Raymond A. Spruance, were enlisted by Lansdale in a plot to poison Recto. In October 1960, while Recto was on a trip to Italy, he had an appointment for coffee with two unidentified Americans in Rome, after which Recto suddenly died. It was described as a heart attack.

One might wish there was a happy ending to the story of Cheez, who was then just 33 years old, with a pretty young wife and son urgently needing his presence and attention. But the last we know is that on October 26, 1951, following the decision of the Philippine Supreme Court, he was released after four years and seven months in prison. Then, instead of being kept under relaxed surveillance and subject to deportation, Cheez simply vanished as he left Bilibad. Which is to say he apparently vanished. Nobody met him at the gate. Not even his old 'friend' Captain Lucero. No journalist showed up, saw him walk away, took notice, or jotted down where he went -- or even that he went somewhere. He was never seen or heard from again by his wife Nina, or by his son Georgie. This is very odd, given that his life until that moment was recorded in excruciating detail by U.S. Counter-Intelligence, by everyone working at the Manila Hotel, by so many newspapers, policemen, secret agents, and informers. Cheez simply disappeared suddenly off the face of the earth. Or was made to disappear.

Looking back upon that strange event, one might wish that he found true refuge somewhere, escaping from the purgatory of paradise. Some might prefer to believe that Claro Recto, understanding the malice at work, had someone meet Cheez as he emerged from the stinking squalor of Bilibad, and saw to it that he was taken to safety elsewhere in the archipelago, where he was reunited with hope, if not with Esperanza, or Nina and Georgie. Were that the case, Recto certainly would have arranged for Nina and Georgie to be brought to his sanctuary, because Cheez obviously loved them dearly.

Sadly, it is more likely that he was met at the gate by Napoleon Valeriano, who took him on a one-way helicopter ride out over the South China Sea. An American CIA agent who had worked with him at G-2 described to us Lansdale's favorite means of execution, which was later adopted by military regimes around the world:

"You don't want to know. It is horrific. The victim -- more often than not an innocent man -- was doped to keep him placid, bound hand and foot with cuffs, then put aboard a chopper at Clark, and flown out over the South China Sea, which took only minutes. At around 2,000 feet altitude, the cuffs were removed, the victim given an intravenous shot of caffeine to wake him. Then he was dragged to the open door and given a long look down. Before he could react to the shock and fear, the soldiers holding him would shove him out, and watch closely while he fell, so they could give Lansdale a full description of the final moments. Incidentally, just before they throw you out, they stab you in the stomach so the gas of decay in your body won't float you to the surface."

Whatever his fate, Cheez ultimately became a cause-celebre, setting precedents for human rights cases not only in Philippine law but in the United Nations. The last word on Cheez comes half a century later from a Manila courthouse decision on August 3, 2107, in a long overdue judgement establishing the human rights of foreign nationals in The Philippines. In his decision, Judge Carpio Morales refers to the landmark case of Vadim Nikolaevich Chirskoff and declares with finality that Cheez had been a "stateless foreign national ... not an enemy".

Unfortunately the official version of Cheez's life, a septic misconstruction born in the mind of Edward G. Lansdale and his spawn in the Counter-Intelligence Corps, and the CIA, remains enshrined forever in the United States National Archives, alongside those other much-abused documents, the Declaration of Independence, the Constitution, and the Bill of Rights.

Epilogue :

HOMEWARD BOUND

Phil had made good his escape to Shanghai, but he was not yet free from ending his life similarly. Because he had been smuggled into China posing as an ATC officer, he risked being caught by the Chinese or by the U.S. Army, who were alerted by authorities at Clark Field. Barely a week after his arrival in Shanghai, he was interviewed by an Army CID agent, but revealed nothing. He did learn a few things. Some friends who had helped him were under investigation, including Bishop Binsted. There was little they could do to the bishop for being kind, since he had not played a direct role in Phil's escape. Nor could they cause problems for Australian Commander Keating. But Babs Limoglia, who was only a secretary at Clark Field, was questioned repeatedly, with hostility. As Phil had torn up the false travel orders Babs prepared, there was nothing the Army could do except warn her she might lose her job.

Phil was waiting in Shanghai for Winkelman's return from San Francisco. As Winkelman had instructed, Dr. Samet was paying Phil a modest salary, which was more than adequate per diem by Chinese standards.

"Peterson worked each day, so I had the use of his Indian Chief motorcycle whenever I wanted it. After typhoons, jungle hammocks, and foul jail cells, the tranquility of life in Shanghai was wonderful."

Phil was living in the YMCA, a popular residence for foreigners with a swimming pool, a gym, and interesting characters in the lobby. One of them was Bill Chang, editor of The China Press, who listened with fascination as Phil recounted his misadventures in The Philippines.

As Mao's Peoples Liberation Army approached Shanghai, the Nationalists were preparing to flee to Taiwan. Everyone knew the old way of life was about to undergo radical change. Many foreign companies were also getting out.

Winkelman returned and, after some heated arguments, Phil agreed to be paid in installments over coming months through Winkelman's bank in San Francisco.

The prospect of going home looked good. Peterson's wife, Kitty, had already left for the States, and Pete was to meet her in San Francisco before going on by car to his home state of Pennsylvania. Bill Chang quit as editor of The China Press and was heading for Honolulu, then the States. Phil decided to accompany Chang. They both bought tickets from China National Airways, which still accepted the almost worthless Nationalist currency. When the aircraft touched down in Honolulu, they had to clear immigration and customs before continuing to the continental United States.

As Phil passed nervously through immigration, his passport was seized by an inspector and he was led to an interrogation room.

"An official told me my passport was out of order because it showed me entering The Philippines twice but not leaving it twice, and leaving China twice but not entering it twice. These irregularities gave him no alternative but to follow the law and send me back to The Philippines. I was in shock."

Bill Chang had seen Phil being led away. When he did not return, Chang found the CNA pilot who had just flown them across the Pacific. He knew the pilot well, because they had all stayed in the YMCA. The pilot was also a friend of Phil's, and knew all the reasons behind his escape from Manila. The pilot went directly to the chief of immigration, and explained why sending this young U.S. Army veteran back to The Philippines would be like "pushing him out a plane over the mid-Pacific". The graphic image worked, and the official decided to overlook Phil's irregularities. The experience was sobering.

After nearly two years in the South Pacific, Phil returned to Palos Verdes briefly in December 1947, where he was happily reunited with his mother and father, sisters and brother.

Peterson soon followed. As a skilled engineer, Pete had already been promised a job with Cooper & Bessemer Machine Company, in Grove City, Pennsylvania, near his home town of Meadville. He and Kitty invited Phil to drive across country in a new Chevy convertible. There was still a lot to talk about.

Reaching Meadville in February, in an icy Pennsylvania winter, the newlyweds rented an apartment in Grove City, Phil sleeping on the sofa.

Cooper & Bessemer was about to install huge engines all over the world, and Pete was to be groomed to head the project. Phil got temporary work there, and moved into an apartment of his own, to spend some months with Pete and Kitty before going home to stay. He had just turned 23, and when it came to conquering new worlds, he wanted to start with Southern California. He was back in Palos Verdes for Christmas, this time for good.

As an epitaph for Cheez, let it be noted that Lansdale's persecution of the Huks failed, as his psychotic deaths squads ultimately failed in other countries. By the early 1950s, the land reform movement in The Philippines had grown to 15,000 men and women in arms in the four central provinces of Pampanga, Nueva Ecija, Tarlac, and Bulacan. All efforts to suppress them failed. Meanwhile the terrible agrarian conditions in The Philippines worsened, by the abuse of U.S. corporations and a ruling Filipino oligarchy who controlled the government through rigged elections bankrolled by Washington.

In 1969, the Huks joined other militant protest groups throughout the archipelago to form a full-fledged revolutionary movement called the New Peoples Army (NPA), which remains a significant force to this day, still without ever receiving any tangible or actual support from Russia.

Officials condemn the NPA as Marxist terrorists, while condemning the Islamic independence movement in Mindanao and the islands of the Sulu Sea as Islamic "terrorists". (In fact, both rebel groups have an "understanding" with the Filipino armed forces, and often stage false battles.) It is all a charade by spin doctors on all sides.

The Pentagon was forced to give up its leases on Clark air base and Subic naval base long ago, because of popular protest. But American financial control of The Philippines is still total.

Soon after returning to live in California, Phil went into the real estate business. While showing a house to clients one day, he met a stunning young woman named Iris-Marie. It was love at first lightning clap. Since then, they have produced a family, and made the kind of money Phil only dreamed about in the Philippines. They built and own a shopping mall; live in a beautiful house by the beach; have friends ranging from famous movie producers like Marty Katz to famous authors and historians like Hampton Sides. They have kept many of their friends in the Philippines, and pitch in earnestly each year to make a success of reunions by the Battling Bastards of Bataan and other famous veterans and victims of World War II in Asia and the Pacific. They also manage to get in a few tangos and waltzes at ballrooms each Saturday Night. Magellan should have had it so good.

Praise for the Seagraves' books

GOLD WARRIORS

"The Seagraves have uncovered one of the biggest secrets of the Twentieth Century."
  -- Iris Chang, author of *The Rape of Nanking*

"Easily the best guide available to the scandal of Yamashita's Gold."
  -- Chalmers Johnson, *London Review of Books*

"The reader will walk away ... astounded and outraged at the immensity of the fraud the world's governments, banks,
and spies are engaged in. ...chilling in its accumulation."
  -- *Counterpunch*

DRAGON LADY

"...unusually gripping... Fascinating in equal measure in is its discussion of Chinese and of English society."
  -- Christopher Hitchens

Its strengths are the color and drama of Tzu Hsi's story itself, Seagraves diligence in scouring a huge variety of sources, and his vivid style."
  -- *The Washington Post*

THE SOONG DYNASTY

"...a gripping account of epochal events ... a marvelous job."
  -- Frank Ching, *The Wall Street Journal*

"...absolutely fascinating... A tremendous though tragic story, marvelously told."
  -- Harvard Professor Edwin O. Reischauer

"The Seagraves write with the assurance, wit and irony that derive from expert knowledge of Chinese history."
-- Anthony Burgess, *London Observer*

THE YAMATO DYNASTY

"...dramatically brings the imperial family -- and those behind it – to life ... An intriguing glimpse behind the ... veil of secrecy."
-- *Publishers Weekly* (starred review)

Printed in Great Britain
by Amazon